Know Your Options

How to Build Wealth Using Proven Options Trading Strategies and Technical Analysis

Bob Lang and Monika Jansen

© 2018 Bob Lang and Monika Jansen
All rights reserved.
ISBN: 1548302651
ISBN-13: 9781548302658

Table of Contents

Introduction 1
Trading as a Metaphor for Life 5
Be Prepared for Anything, or What to Expect 11
Psychology of Trading: How to Prepare Mentally 19
Take Your Charts to Heart: How to Analyze
Technical Patterns 27
Turn Down the Noise: How to Manage the Media 43
The Art of Selling 47
Save Yourself: The Principles of Risk Management 49
Price and Volume: Two Key Technical Elements 55
Option Flow: Follow the Big Money 61
Market Sentiment: Indicators and How to Use Them 67
Pricing Options: Implied Versus Historical Volatility 75
Options 101 81
Options 201 91
Options 301 105
Listen to and Learn from the Pros 115
Ready to Trade? You Need to Fill Your Toolbox 145
My Reading List 149
Case Studies 155
The Mad Money Experience 165
Glossary 169
Acknowledgments 181
About the Authors 183

Praise

Bob Lang shares his hard-earned experience after more than two decades in the options market. He shows you all the common pitfalls of options trading, and how to avoid them. You don't have to go it alone! Whether you're a seasoned trader or a newbie who wants to learn how a put differs from a call, Bob is your expert and approachable guide every step of the way. – **Kate Stalter, Financial Advisor and Author**

Love that "Know your Options" offers readers the gritty truths of trading options. Bob Lang offers an impressive array of well-organized and well-thought out tips and tricks to improving the odds of stock options trading success. Trading profitably isn't easy but it isn't impossible either. Regardless of your experience and skill level, if you are interested in approaching the financial markets with a practical and realistic approach, this book is a must read! – **Carley Garner, commodity market strategist, futures and options broker and author, Higher Probability Commodity Trading**

In "Know Your Options," Bob Lang offers timely and compelling content that will prove highly useful to all traders, and especially to those who want to trade options. Bob and Monika's writing style is clear, concise and easy-to-understand. I especially enjoyed his trading examples and his common-sense advice about risk-management. If you want to gain a better understanding of how to approach the market and how to trade options successfully—read this book! – **Toni Turner, author, A Beginner's Guide to Day Trading Online, 2nd Ed.**

Bob Lang has succeeded in assembling a comprehensive road map for options traders, and his new book, "Know Your Options," provides sound options trading information from start to finish. Best of all, Bob and his co-author Monika Jansen get right to point, delivering key concepts in an accurate and concise manner. Whether you're seeking strategies for profit or protection, you'll find them in "Know Your Options." – **Ed Ponsi, author, Technical Analysis and Chart Interpretations**

Free Gift

As a big thank you to our readers, we'd like to offer you a free gift. Click on the link below to sign up for our 10-Day Trader Challenge.

Each day, you'll receive an email that introduces you to a concept that's important in options trading – and to your long-term success as an options trader. You'll learn:

- How to prepare mentally
- The fundamentals of risk management
- Basic technical patterns every trader must know
- The top indicators to follow
- And MUCH MORE!

To receive your free gift, sign up at:

http://eepurl.com/dhL4iX

1

Foreword

There are millions of traders and investors trying to secure their financial future by taking control of their investments. Sadly, most of them will fail. Although traders now have access to the tools that they needed to be successful, the right tools are not enough. Temperament, discipline, focus and knowing what tools and trading style are right for you, will determine whether you will be a profitable trader or one of the 95% that do not.

In Know Your Options, my good friend Bob Lang and his editor Monika Jansen take us on a journey that spans a 25-year trading career, as he shares the accumulated knowledge that has made him the successful trader that he is today.

In the five years that Bob and I have worked together, I have developed a deep respect for his integrity and his dedication to educating traders. His willingness to share his knowledge permeates this book.

Whereas most investment books foster the idea that there is a "holy grail" for making money in the stock and options market, Bob knows better. The book begins by focusing us on the building blocks of profitable trading: Preparation, Consistency and Protection of Capital, and then proceeds to the importance of technical analysis, encouraging us to ignore the headlines while focusing on the power of price action as a guide to profitable trades.

Further down this path we learn the importance of risk management, diversification, money management and knowing when to sell. It is only after he has built this solid foundation of best practices that Bob gets into the specifics of options trading. After showing us the importance of big money options order flow, Bob's particular area of expertise, we learn the basics of options trading, leaning heavily of technical analysis to define trends and entry points, and moving on to advanced options strategies.

The book, which intersperses wisdom of some of the most successful investors in Wall Street history, ends with anecdotes from some of the people, like Jim Cramer, who have influenced Bob on his journey to consistent options profits.

Marc Chaikin
Founder and CEO, Chaikin Analytics LLC
January 2018

Introduction

You have heard the stories of investors who accumulate vast amounts of wealth in the stock market. Some get rich during market crashes and others take advantage of long bull runs when the markets do nothing but move higher.

One of the best-known crashes in modern history occurred on October 19, 1987, when the Dow Industrials fell a stunning 22.6%. "Black Monday" devastated many investors and put several completely out of business.

Yet, some very savvy investors, like famed trader Paul Tudor Jones, took advantage of the situation and not only made big money on the move down but also rode the bounce back up. (After such a spectacular drop the markets recovered 85% of those losses in just two short weeks!) He was able to remain flexible and use derivatives like options and futures to leverage huge returns for his fund and his clients.

During the very long bull run that began in 2009 and continues as of this writing, you may have watched your brother-in-law accumulate stupid amounts of wealth. He got in on the right stocks at the right time – and got out from the right stocks at the right time.

Like a moth attracted to the flame, you want in. The idea of trading the markets is attractive. There is no manual labor involved and the hours are ideal (depending on your time zone).

Do some research, put your capital to work, and you'll make it happen. It'll be easy, right?

I hate to break it to you, but unfortunately there is no easy way to make money in the stock market. No one has written the "silver bullet" guide, manual, or handbook that teaches you all of the skills necessary to make one winning trade after another and hit it big (mostly because that would be impossible!).

Furthermore, trading can be a lonely business. It's just you and your computer or mobile device. So, who can you turn to for guidance? Who can help you think through a trade in a tough situation? It's every man for himself (and every woman for herself).

The reality is, your chance of successfully trading the markets over the long-term without a commitment to education, honing your skills, and learning from your experience is close to nil. And that's why I wrote this book.

I started trading options more than 20 years ago. I've made every mistake in the book – and learned from them. I developed my technical skills and charting expertise so I could make informed trading decisions based on what the market was telling me. I learned to ignore the talking heads and read indicators. I've read and studied a lot – I still do. And I polished strategies for successfully trading options over the long-term.

This book contains all of the knowledge I've accumulated over the years. You will learn new skills and strategies. You will learn how to be accountable and manage risk responsibly. You will learn how to admit you're wrong so you stay in the game.

You will learn that ego has no place in trading and that the market will humble you – quickly.

You will also learn how to overcome psychological barriers. Options trading is a mental game. You need to stay focused if you want to be a successful options trader over the long-term.

When you finish reading this book, you will be ready to trade options for income. You will understand the ins and outs of options trading, technical analysis and risk management. You will use everything you learned on a regular basis. You will be able to create an action plan and feedback mechanisms that are critical to your success.

Good luck!

Your friend in trading,
Bob Lang

CHAPTER 1

Trading as a Metaphor for Life

> *"I made a killing in the stock market. My broker lost all my money, so I killed him."*
>
> *– Jim Loy*

The life of a trader is similar to an athlete's. You practice, practice, and practice some more. You learn from your mistakes. You learn how to manage risk and emotions. You learn how to overcome challenges that pop up due to your own short-comings or the actions of opponents. Finally, you make it into the big leagues, where all of that practice will (hopefully) translate into success and long-term survival.

Survival? You might think I'm exaggerating, but options trading for income is truly about survival. Unlike many careers that provide some guarantee of certainty (meteorologists know the weather will change, supermarkets know people will need food, CPAs know people need to pay taxes every year), there is no such thing in the trading world. You must rely on your instincts, protect your capital, and constantly search for new opportunities. You are always trying to improve your profit and loss (P&L) statement; in fact, this is your scorecard. If you have too many days when the "L" is greater than the "P," you'll find yourself on the sidelines and out of the action – perhaps permanently.

Managing your emotional highs and lows is key to surviving, and it hinges on your ability to control your fear and greed. These are emotions each of us humans share, and they can get the better of us. When it comes to money, we want to accumulate more but we are always fearful of losing what we have. This can cloud your judgment very easily, cause you to follow the herd, and ruin your performance. In a 2002 study done by Michael Mauboussin of Credit Suisse, he noted, "Markets tend to function well when a sufficient number of diverse investors interact. Conversely, markets tend to become fragile when this diversity breaks down and investors act in a similar way."

Survival is also about knowing the odds and placing your bets on the highest probabilities. Your assessment of the risk in each situation is crucial to continuing your journey as a trader. There are no guarantees here, but if you put yourself in the best position to succeed, you at least have a sporting chance. If you do not know the odds and place a bet anyway, you're playing a guessing game. Over the long run, you will lose.

I know of some options traders who manage risk by **making a market.** This means they create a buy or sell environment and take on the risk that buyers or sellers will show up. When they do so, they'll hedge their bets with opposing positions, some of which are just extraordinary in size. While this is a "steadier" way of trading – you do much of the work to remove the risk – the potential payoff is limited. Yes, you can win bets in this fashion, but how many of us have an enormous pool of money to work with?

The vast majority of traders are not that conservative. If you want to trade over the long term, you should use disciplined risk management techniques (we'll cover risk management in chapter 7), swing for singles or doubles, and be surprised when you hit a homerun every once in a while.

In my years of trading, I have seen the rise and fall of many, many traders. Some have accumulated enormous fortunes from a very humble, small stake. Some have crashed and burned by taking on too much risk, letting their emotions get the best of them, or being in the wrong place at the wrong time. Talent notwithstanding, timing and unforeseen circumstances often dictate the final outcome. Just like in a championship sports game, the winner and loser may be separated by one blink-and-you- missed-it play.

If you want to succeed as an options trader, the key to wealth building is not to hedge your bets constantly. Instead, you want to use tools, techniques, philosophies, experience and instinct to place *directional* bets (betting on which way the stock market is going – up or down). A trader can win playing both bull and bear sides, but let's face facts: the long-term trend of the stock market is up. Play in that direction over a long stretch of time, and you will be a winner.

Now, I'm not saying that options trading is that simple. Trading is not a game of perfect, but like a baseball player who can make millions for failing to hit the ball seven out of ten times, an options trader can show positive P&L with less than a 50% win rate. It's not easy, but these traders tend to manage winning and losing trades in much the same way that they handle life's challenges. Prior experiences inform the choices they make. There is no guarantee that your choice will be a successful, but the probability is in your favor.

At this point, you probably understand that risk management is a discipline that is critical to survival. It is easy to forget the principles of risk management when you're in the heat of battle, but it is those who are most disciplined that tend to survive the ups and downs you face each day as a trader.

I have survived as a trader by meeting challenges head on, committing to constantly learning and growing, and thinking about the long-term, big picture: retirement. One of the biggest challenge all of us face is accumulating enough wealth so we can retire if we so choose. The problems with Social Security are well documented; there are no guarantees we will receive back what we pay into it upon retirement. Therefore, we must take responsibility and a "risk on" approach to grow our wealth now – not at retirement.

Luckily, historical precedent is on your side. Since 1928, the average annual return on the SPX 500 has been 10% (per investopedia.com). Leaving your money invested in stocks yields a compounded doubling of your money within 10 years. By comparison, investing in 10-year treasury bonds, a less risky investment, yields about half as much (5.2%), and investing in 3-month treasury bills has an even lower return (3.5%).

Consider this scenario:

You invest $25,000 in the US stock market. After 30 years, you would have around $436,000. If you invested that same amount of money over the same amount of time in 10 year treasuries, you'd only have $117,000. You get paid for taking risk. Investing in the stock market is hands down the best way to grow wealth over a longer period of time.

Trading is a journey that is filled with painful and pleasurable experiences – there is no getting around this reality. Want to avoid these experiences completely? Put all of your money in the bank and forget about it. That should be the safest move, right? Yet, as we found out during the 2008 global financial crisis, even that conservative approach was not a guarantee of capital return.

If you play the game right and learn the tricks to surviving – and thriving – as an options trader, the **stock market** provides a mechanism to increase wealth like no other, period. Welcome to options trading.

I first learned about the importance of saving and **investing** at a very young age. My parents were savers, and they taught my brother and I the value of discipline and responsibility. We lived in a tight-knit, middle class community in Los Angeles that was surrounded by substantial wealth (Beverly Hills, Brentwood, Santa Monica, and Pacific Palisades), but we never felt "not rich" enough.

My dad was a broker from the early 1960's until the mid 1970's. He had learned the value of building wealth via investing from his own family, which had built a nice fortune during the post-WWII boom. Back then, if you bought stock in a company, your intention was to hold it forever and perhaps pass it on to the next generation. Even Warren Buffett says his goal is to buy companies he would hold forever.

While that strategy may have been a winning one in the early to mid-20th century, today's market requires a different strategic plan. The "buy and hold" mantra of the past can very easily turn into "hope and pray."

Before we move on, I have a little story for you. My first foray into investing came in 1981 when I was in eighth grade. My history teacher, Mr. Jensen, had an open stock market contest (frankly, I think he was just looking for stock tips for himself!). Well, knowing my dad had experience in the stock market, I thought first prize would be a slam dunk for me. My dad suggested I buy Halliburton, the oil services company. It did very well, but not well enough. I came in fourth. My good friend Rebecca Slater won with her pick of Fluor. That was my first tough loss – but I survived.

Chapter 1 Takeaways

- *In trading as in life, you have to be on your toes and ready for whatever comes.*

- *Your trading career could be a long one if you check your ego at the door.*

- *Taking on risk is part of investing world, so good risk management is critical to survival.*

CHAPTER 2

Be Prepared for Anything, or What to Expect

"Ninety percent of the people in the stock market, professionals and amateurs alike, simply haven't done enough homework."

– William O'Neill

Imagine waking up one morning for yet another day in your life as a trader. You check pre-market reports, look up the Nikkei and Euro, and scan the news. The markets are kind of quiet. You have some nice positions on good names, and things are just floating along smoothly.

Then an unforeseen, absolutely catastrophic event turns the world upside down, and your quiet day comes crashing down around you.

Welcome to every trader's experience on September 11, 2001.

Preparation is key if you want to be ready for everything and anything that comes your way. In trading, there is *always* uncertainty. Nobody can consistently predict future outcomes, but we can prepare ourselves for whatever those outcomes are by learning, practicing, and putting backup plans in place.

Let's be honest here: Trading is definitely not an easy way to make money. It's challenging and gratifying, nerve-wracking and euphoria-inducing – sometimes all in the same day.

Many traders base their success on the strength of their bottom line, which makes sense – but that's only part of the story. Growing wealth is important, but for me, being a successful trader is about sustainability, longevity, and consistency. If you said to me, "Bob, I grew my options trading account by 100% in a month!" I would say, "Well, that is quite a feat, but let's see positive results next month, the month after that, in one year, and in five years."

CONSISTENT RESULTS BUILD WEALTH

While a good month may include hard work and even some luck, achieving success month after month requires careful preparation so you can successfully trade any outcome. For traders, preparation means *taking action based on your experience.*

Experience is a major factor for your success. Each trade brings another opportunity for you to learn, improve, and write your own "book of trading." The more trades you make, the larger your book. You will also write pages as you observe markets, watch how news affects your positions, bank wins and suffer losses.

The best traders are constantly learning how to improve their strategy. They are sponges, soaking up information from articles and books, eager to use the best tools and techniques, and open to learning from the mistakes of others.

Knowledge and experience are a powerful combination. You will try new strategies based on what you learn and observe, you will note what works and what doesn't, and you will begin to save yourself from disastrous outcomes.

Here are my tips on how to prepare for anything.

DO YOUR HOMEWORK

I'm a big fan of Jim Cramer's mantra, "Do your homework." A technical analyst will study charts, indicators, momentum and volume trends. A fundamental analyst will dig into earnings, sales, the macro environment, and valuation A full- time market watcher will monitor the action all day long, learning and watching for developments.

The 2002 World Series of Poker champion Robert Varkonyi once said, "No-limit hold 'em is hours and hours of boredom and moments of sheer terror." He might as well have been talking about trading. As a trader, you generally sit around and wait for something to happen, but if you're smart, you are also constantly learning. You're reading the news, listening to interviews, checking the charts and technicals, and sizing up the market. Remember, knowledge is power. The more you know, the better prepared you will be for any outcome.

STUDY MORE THAN YOU THINK YOU NEED TO

You probably allocate some time to studying before markets open and after they close, which is great. By studying, I mean researching companies, finding the best chart setups, learning about different technical patterns and applying those skills to make the best probable trades or investments.

But what if you pushed yourself to do more? What if you studied for 30 more minutes each day? That's 2 1/2 hours more per week and an extra 10 hours per month. String that out over a year, and you have put in an extra 120 hours (or five days) of studying! Think of the edge you will have over the rest of the crowd – you will be much better prepared.

What if you take it a step further? What if you cut back on activities that are complete time wasters? Think about what will give you the best "bang for your time." It's not checking Facebook every 30 minutes or watching SportsCenter twice a day. Time wasted will never be returned – but it will put us behind and leave us less prepared. Instead, use that time for learning.

I recommend that my clients, coaching students and subscribers read more. Find the best sources of information, maximize social media (there is always someone out there who knows more than you do!), and ask questions constantly.

PRACTICE

As the saying goes, practice makes perfect. Michael Jordan once said, "I play to win, whether during practice or a real game. And I will not let anything get in the way of me and my competitive enthusiasm to win."

If you are not ready to trade with real money, don't. For traders just starting out, I always suggest practicing on paper, where you can safely experiment with different trades and strategies. Create a trading plan, follow it, track your successes and failures and learn what works and doesn't work

The lessons learned from losing money can sting badly, and once you lose money it becomes difficult to recover it (see the table below). Imagine losing 50% of your capital – you would need to gain 100% on the remaining amount just to get back to breakeven! By trading on paper, you'll learn quickly how your mind handles wins and losses (but without the fear of losing real money).

JOIN A COMMUNITY

A full-time trader usually works alone. Because it's just you and the markets, I often compare trading to surfing. You've got nothing but your surfboard, instincts, and experience to help you survive. When your session is over, you want to return to shore safely.

Likewise, traders want to finish the day feeling good – and with more profits than losses. Imagine how much easier and less uncertain it would be if you could tap into the collective experience of others?

When I started the Explosive Options chat service in July 2013, I made the commitment to provide support and encouragement to all members – novice or experienced – and help them "learn while they earn."

Our room has been a resounding success for all members. The most satisfying part is the strong sense of community. We are learning and striving to get better. While there is no better teacher than a trading day, knowing we're all in it together – and want to help each other – makes trading that much easier.

You don't have to join our chat room (though you are more than welcome to!), but I would encourage you to join one. There truly is strength in numbers, and I cannot think of a better way to prepare for success as a trader than by actively learning from others.

BE PATIENT

Look at what happened during the **Great Recession** of 2008-09. The stock market melted down in six short months as easily as a hot knife slices through butter. Nothing was spared from the carnage. The selling was so intense it took down not only stocks but commodities, futures, and even so-called safe haven investments like municipal bonds.

Sizeable investments that people had held for decades were chopped in half – or worse. Life savings vaporized. **401K plans** were cut mercilessly. Investors were left wondering if any of their companies would survive, let alone rise again.

As we all remember, banks were brought to their knees and suddenly faced bankruptcy or even government conservatorship. Bank of America fell from the $40 range to nearly $3 per share, losing close to 95% of its value. Goldman Sachs fell about 60% from its highs. AIG, the world's largest insurance company, lost 95% of its value before the Federal government stepped in with emergency assistance. Citigroup lost nearly 98% of its value.

Meanwhile, the media was telling investors to buy these names, as this was going to be a once in a lifetime chance to get on board. "Buy it now, and just hold it forever!" Well, that turned out to be very poor advice in most cases, as there were more painful declines to come. This was not a time to buy low.

This was a time when you would have been better off just waiting.

The **opportunity cost** of buying too early was extremely high, as it forced you into a hope and pray mode of thinking. Of course, you might be thinking, "But hindsight is 20/20. How could anyone have known at the time that stocks would fall so far?" And you would be mostly right. No one knew.

However, if you had been patient, used your common sense, and listened to the markets at a time when panic was rampant, you could have made that "once in a lifetime" trade work for you. Buffett tells us to "be greedy when others are fearful, be fearful when others are greedy." That is great advice that I try to keep in mind.

Buy and hold is no longer a solid strategy due to the extreme volatility that is present in markets. You cannot buy today, wake up 20 years from now and only then decide to look at your portfolio. Do you really want to hope and pray that things get better? Definitely not.

The name of the game today is timing the market. Pay attention and make trades that respond to the message of the markets.

Chapter 2 Takeaways

- *Producing consistent results is the key to building wealth*

- *Commit to learning – it's one of the best ways to become a successful trader.*

- *Practice makes perfect, especially in trading.*

- *The old days of buy and hold investing are long gone.*

- *Opportunity cost is high if you become greedy or complacent.*

- *The Great Recession taught us that being patient and thoughtful can give you an edge.*

CHAPTER 3

Psychology of Trading: How to Prepare Mentally

> *"Emotions are your worst enemy in the stock market."*
>
> *– Don Hays*

In the previous chapter, I discussed the importance of preparation; specifically how knowledge and experience work hand-in-hand to ensure you can handle any trading situation that's thrown at you. Knowledge and experience will get you far, but if you don't understand the psychology of trading and how to keep your head in the game when the stakes are high, your career might be very short-lived.

I cannot underestimate the importance of mindset when it comes to trading. It is critical that our minds are ready, willing, and able to face each new day. Markets have no memory, which means we start from scratch each trading day. It takes nerves of steel to handle the constant up-and-down of the markets. So, I have to ask:

- Are you mentally prepared to absorb shocking news that could rock the financial markets?

- Could you stay calm, cool, and collected to ensure your portfolio isn't decimated in one day?

- Can you be clear-headed enough to find the right time to exit trades while looking for new opportunities to buy?

WELCOME TO A WORLD GOVERNED BY FEAR AND GREED

The good news is that only two emotions govern traders: fear and greed. If you can learn how to manage your emotions and keep greed and fear in check, you can survive as a trader. (More good news: you can actually see fear and greed play out in charts, but we'll cover that later.)

Just as the sun rises in the east and sets in the west, a trader's emotions ride along the spectrum of fear and greed. These are constants, and because we're humans, they are psychological barriers that we are bound to. There will be days when you become emotionally overwhelmed and fear or greed drive you to make poor decisions. It will happen to you – I promise you that!

(I would be remiss if I didn't mention some other emotions traders often experience. At various times, you will feel doubt, regret, anger, isolation – but you'll also experience elation and pride.)

You might wonder why there's only two emotions you need to worry about when trading, but it's pretty straightforward. You fear losing your money. When you're living in a fearful state, you become more risk averse, scared to buy options and scared to sell. You end up paralyzed as opportunities pass you by, and your portfolio suffers as a result.

You are also greedy when it comes to money. You want more, more, more! When you're governed by greed, you'll push the envelope and take on risk (sometimes too much) in order to build your stack of cash even higher. Of course, I don't need to tell you that putting too many eggs in one basket is a bad idea, nor do I need to tell you what can happen to your portfolio if that trade goes south.

It is imperative that no matter which emotions are coursing through your veins, you react appropriately. But there's a twist: you also have to understand what everyone else is feeling and where they are on the fear-greed spectrum. By reading the markets, you will have an advantage. It's not as hard as it sounds (we'll cover how to read emotions in charts later).

In trading, it's important to understand that there is a herd mentality. Just like sheep, cows, and other livestock, humans want to be together, whether the direction we are moving in is right or wrong. It is considered safer to be with the crowd than all alone. Unfortunately, that mentality is not always healthy.

A one-day sharp move down in the markets is hardly ever anticipated, yet many traders will panic and throw in the towel at precisely the wrong time. On the flip side, when a market moves sharply higher, traders who are sitting on the sidelines (without any trades in play) feel left out. They missed a rally! It is frustrating, but unfortunately, that frustration gets the best of them, and they will buy options when bullish sentiment is far too high.

Some traders (myself included) will go completely in the opposite direction of the herd mentality, ignore fear and greed outright, and make contrarian bets. This strategy is often rewarded, but you have to know what you're doing. I use sentiment tools to measure where money is flowing, and frankly, it's not difficult to decipher – money either flows into a stock or index, or it flows out. As we will discuss in later chapters, timing these trades is really tough to figure out, but if you play the highest probabilities based on historical outcomes, you often have a winning bet on your hands.

HOW TO HANDLE SURPRISES

Have you ever heard the term "black swan?" It's a metaphor for an event that is as rare as one black swan among a flock of one hundred white swans. In other words, it is an extreme outlier event

As you might guess from the name, a black swan event is a negative event that can potentially cause major market damage (and unfortunately, they have become rather common in the financial markets). The psychological effects from a losing large sums of money very quickly can be unnerving and cause a lot of fear.

Because the global community has become so interconnected, events that occur on the other side of the world can have severe ramifications at home. Examples include the 9/11 terrorist attacks, 2008 financial crisis, 2010 flash crash, Arab Spring uprisings, Fukushima nuclear disaster, and the 2015 European financial crisis that hit Greece and a few other countries particularly hard.

The key to handling black swan events is avoiding complacency. This is easier said than done, because when you are confident about your trading strategy and investments, you relax – sometimes too much. When complacency kicks in, a black swan event will catch you off guard. Unless you have some insurance (we call it protection) in place, you may not be able to respond quickly enough to stem the losses. You will panic and shift into risk aversion mode.

Your reaction is completely rational, but that's beside the point. If you want to increase your wealth while working in an uncertain environment, you will have better luck managing your emotions by reducing your risk.

REDUCE RISK BY BUYING PUTS

Understand that it is nearly impossible to protect against every negative event if you are in wealth-building mode. You cannot build wealth without taking on some risk, but you hedge your risk. One strategy is to buy options on both sides of the trade, which is akin to betting on both teams playing in this weekend's big football game (but with no point spread). Yes, it reduces your potential profits, but it also reduces your potential losses.

As an investor, what you really want is maximum returns with less risk – we all do. That is the ideal combination, but black swan events put your capital at risk – even if you're making "safe" bets. Market risk always includes a premium based on volatility; volatility often changes over a certain time period (called the standard deviation). Luckily, you can reduce overall market risk and the effects of volatility by adding protection to your portfolio – but this only works for long-term plays, not short-term

Here's how it works: Buy put premium on long-term (bullish or bearish) plays, which will shield your portfolio in case the stock market falls sharply. It's very similar to buying an insurance policy for your home – you're only rewarded if disaster strikes. While paying for this premium will reduce your overall return (insurance is not free!), the price will reduce the potential effects of market volatility and it will allow you to sleep better.

Even if you're invested for the long haul – 30 years or more – and know that the odds of a rising stock market are in your favor, markets will correct (aka, take a nose-dive and drop hundreds of points). Your mind will run through every painful emotional response out there. Do you really want to place yourself in a position of fear? Of course not!

Markets today act differently than they did in the past. This is definitely not your grandfather's market. There are more participants, more global events, more companies in a more connected world that is constantly changing. One day you may be comfortably invested in a multibillion dollar firm, and the next month it could be brought to its knees – with your investment completely wiped out.

Now, the odds of that happening are indeed long, but they're certainly possible. There is absolutely no need to place your portfolio at risk or to lose countless hours of sleep. Buy some index put options, which can easily be done within a regular investment account, retirement account or trust account.

During the days, weeks, and months when markets decline or move sideways – and they are plentiful – it will be a great relief to have this protection in place. Put options increase in value if the market declines, which is why buying put options is an inexpensive way of insuring your portfolio against a disastrous market decline.

A savvy investor will have protection at all times. The cost of buying puts should pale in comparison to the overall value of your investment portfolio (just like your monthly homeowner's insurance is a fraction of the overall value of your home).

TWO MORE WAYS TO PROTECT YOUR PORTFOLIO

Another, more conventional way to protect a long portfolio would be to short stocks, specifically indices like the SPX 500, Russell 2000, Nasdaq or Dow Industrials. While the effect is the same as buying puts, the downside is that you need to invest more capital in order to offset the value of a portfolio. Stick with put options.

Then there's cash. Many don't consider cash as an insurance tool, but it is. Cash is psychologically comforting, and it allows you to buy when the right opportunities arise. If you are all in with no cash lying around, you cannot add to your portfolio. To build wealth and take advantage of the power of compound growth, you need to add new positions or build on existing ones. One great way to build cash is by rotating out of names that are not working or cutting back on a position or two that has grown too large.

You'll be most thankful that you have cash on hand during a correction. Case in point: When stocks were dropping like hot potatoes in 2008, numerous investors were all in with no cash to spare. In a few short weeks, the stock market had dropped to levels not seen in twenty years! If you had cash, you were handed the opportunity of a lifetime to buy some truly outstanding stocks. Rule of thumb: Always have some cash at the ready!

Chapter 3 Takeaways

- *Be mentally prepared by understanding black swan events and the consequences of fear and greed.*

- *Reduce risk by adding put options to your portfolio.*

- *Keep cash on hand for the psychological benefit and to buy into new trades when the opportunity arises.*

CHAPTER 4

Take Your Charts to Heart: How to Analyze Technical Patterns

> *"You're neither right nor wrong because other people agree with you.*
>
> *You're right because your facts are right and your reasoning is right – and that's the only thing that makes you right."*
>
> *– Warren Buffett*

Technical analysis and charting is often mistaken for mysterious and mystical practices, like voodoo or tarot cards. In reality, charts offer a look at past behavior, and I can tell you without hesitation that past behavior informs future behavior. Our behavioral patterns are ingrained in our DNA; they never change over time. Every decision we make is based on prior experience.

BEHAVIORAL PSYCHOLOGY AND TRADING

You can learn a lot about trading from behavioral psychologists **Ivan Pavlov** and **B.F. Skinner**. They taught us about:

Classical conditioning: Learning to associate an unconditioned stimulus that already brings about a particular response with a new (conditioned) stimulus, so that the new stimulus brings about the same response.

Operant conditioning: If behavior is reciprocated with a certain consequence, whether it is a positive or a negative reinforcement, the behavior is more likely to be repeated and become constant.

You can use these two theories to discover patterns and trends in stock charts that repeat over and over again. And, you can combine the theories with your knowledge of fear and greed (I covered this in-depth in Chapter 3) to place directional bets via stocks, options, and futures.

(Keep in mind that people rush into fear but not greed. With greed, we will wait for some sort of confirmation before buying. With fear, we will rush for the exits in a stampede. As the old saying goes on Wall Street, *"You take the elevator up and the window down."*)

The chart below shows the dynamics of fear and greed, which you can watch play out in real-time as well.

Simply put, a down session (red bar) indicates fear, while an up session (green bar) indicates greed. The amount of movement indicates the degree of fear or greed (which usually isn't extreme).

TECHNICAL PATTERNS EVERY TRADER MUST KNOW

Your job as a technical analyst is to look for behavioral clues and patterns that occur over and over again and then follow them to place a high probability bet. Markets trend up and down based on the flow of liquidity, which is directly connected to fear and greed. If investors are emboldened and believe the market will rise, more money pours in and prices go up. If investors are worried, money flows out and prices drop.

The notion that the crowd is often late and wrong is something that shows up in sentiment polls, equity flows, and fear/greed indicators. Market corrections happen without much warning; nobody stands out on the street waving a white flag and yelling, "Get out!" There are a million reasons to sell stocks, but only one reason to buy – a stock is going higher.

Some of the most obvious technical patterns can easily be explained by human behavior. Take a **W chart pattern**, a formation that happens when a stock drops to an interim bottom, rallies to resistance, retests that bottom, and then moves past resistance to new highs. The Foot Locker chart below is a great example.

This pattern is simply telling you to only trust the bottom if it is not penetrated. Buying into a decline is painful and highly discouraged unless your timeframe is forever. You want to be risk averse in a down stock or index until you have confidence the trend has changed. The W pattern tends to be a bullish one that plays out in a continuation move as a base is carved out on the right side of the chart.

How about the reverse of the W – the **M pattern**? As you might suspect, this is a bearish pattern that occurs when you see a **double top** forming. Buyers are not interested in paying higher prices twice at the same level; that rejection causes sellers to appear and the pattern is established. Naturally, the downside action often accelerates quickly as fear takes hold.

The **head and shoulders pattern** is one that always needs to be considered. This is a classic trend reversal pattern that is often associated with a bearish follow-on move after the pattern has been established. As we see in the chart below, a high is made (left shoulder) followed by a higher high (head), then a pullback and lower high (right shoulder). Below the two shoulders is the neckline (support). A break of that level is typically a signal that more downside action is coming. A price objective would be the difference between the head and the neckline. In the case of Caterpillar, a break of that neckline around the $69 area projects to around a $4 move to $65.

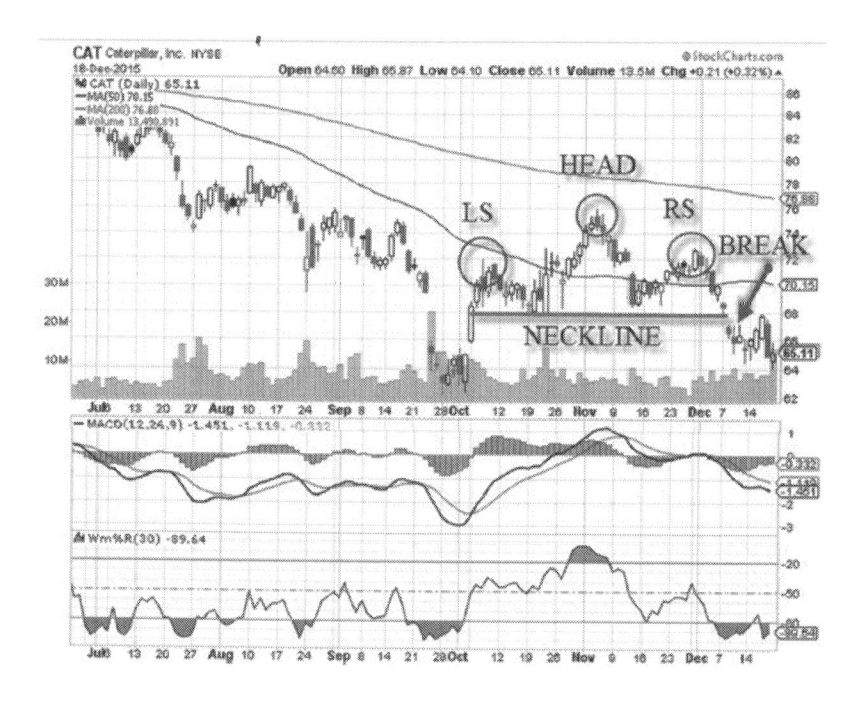

Now, if a head and shoulders pattern is bearish, you should consider the opposite pattern as bullish. An inverse head and shoulders pattern is a reliable pattern that plays out when a price tests a low and makes a higher low pattern on the chart. A break of the neckline is a measured move (difference between the head and the neck-line). In the case of Intel, a move of roughly $3 past the neckline, or nearly $33, completed the pattern.

Moving average crossovers, aka, long term crossovers, must always be respected, as pressure to buy and sell tends to shift trends quickly. Institutional players also pay very close attention to them, which will affect the flow of money. Two classic examples are the golden cross and the death cross.

The **golden cross** happens when the 50-day moving average crosses above the 200-day moving average. It provides long-term fund managers with confidence that the market will move higher. Fifty days is the equivalent of roughly two and a half months, while 200 days is the equivalent of one year (remember, we're talking about trading days – not the calendar year). When a shorter term moving average crosses above the longer term average, it is considered a bullish event by technical analysts. If higher trading volume the same time as a crossover, you have a strong signal that stocks may propel higher.

Conversely, a **death cross** occurs when the 50-day moving average crosses under the 200-day moving average, indicating that prices are going down, at least in the short-term. When this happens, institutions are likely to **distribute** stock (sell long-term holdings) and lock in profits. This event is often viewed as a negative over the long-term, but only if the condition persists or happens when price is well below the moving averages.

There have been times when a death cross was a great buy signal, so the results are somewhat mixed (see chart). However, a death cross normally occurs near the end of a bull cycle, and in fact it's often the final sign that we are shifting into a bear cycle. When price is below the moving averages, you'll see heavy resistance keeping the price down as sellers unload their stock.

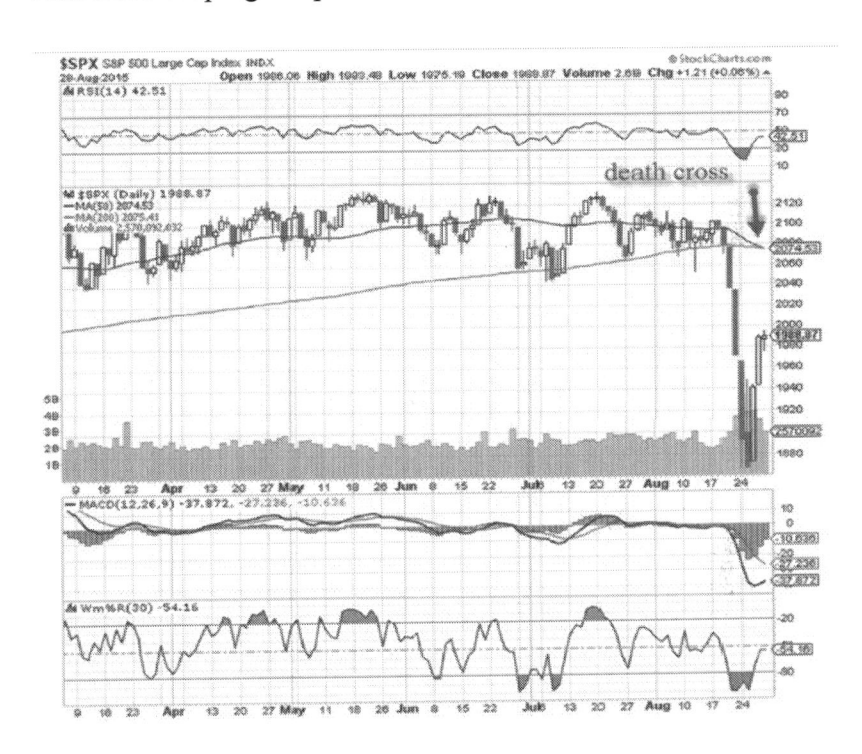

John Bollinger is a legendary contributor to the technical analysis community for creating a valuable tool called **bollinger bands**. These are a simple statistical tool that use probability with data points. A volatility band around the mean (price) shows the probability of where a data point will land. (If you want a more technical explanation: Bollinger bands are an adaptation of keltner bands, envelopes and donchian channels, but bollingers use the purest statistical data to estimate a probable outcome.)

Here's how I use them in a stock chart: I will plot two standard deviations around the mean (bands), because there is a 95% probability that a new price level (daily) will land inside the bands. Since price action is dynamic, the tool takes into consideration volatility.

Bandwidth is an important consideration when analyzing bollinger bands. The dynamics of price will move the bands from wide to narrow, depending on how historical data points move the bands. Narrow bands imply price contraction, and it may signal a large move is coming. In the chart below, note how the narrow bands indicate a decrease in volatility, while the widening bands imply a jump in volatility (or panic) but are generally short term in nature.

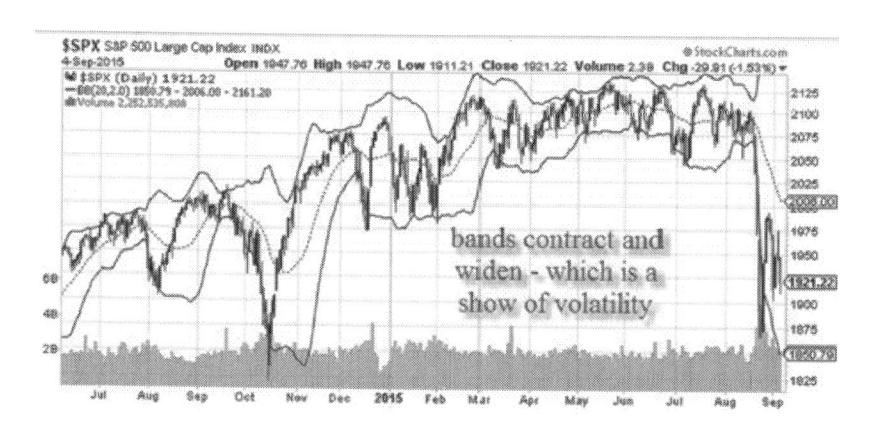

Famed investor George Soros once said, "The biggest profits are made in the **fat tails**." Fat tail events are outliers on the frequency distribution spectrum; they sit in the 5% probability zone. But they do happen! And when they do, you can win – BIG. In fact, as an options trader, you can ride a fat tail for big profits in a very short timeframe. I know it's possible, because I've done it – and not just once.

KNOW YOUR OPTIONS · 37

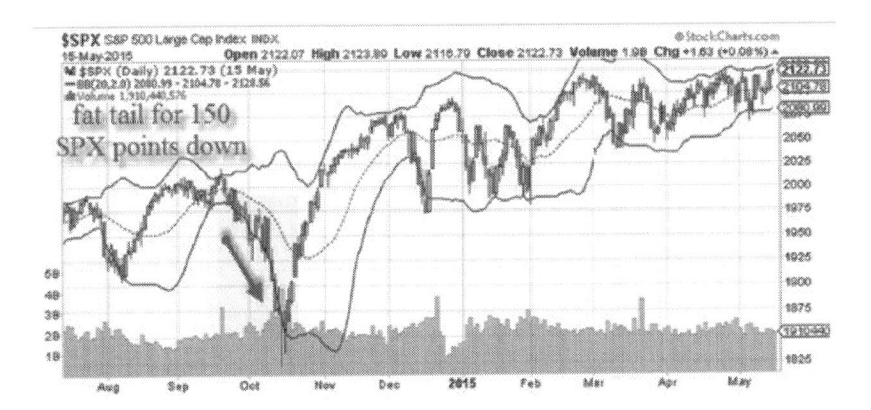

[Chart: $SPX S&P 500 Large Cap Index, 15-May-2015, annotated "fat tail for 150 SPX points down"]

While seemingly rare (especially when you consider that price only lives in the fat tail area 5% of the time), fat tail events happen more frequently than one would believe, and they have a substantial effect on a portfolio.

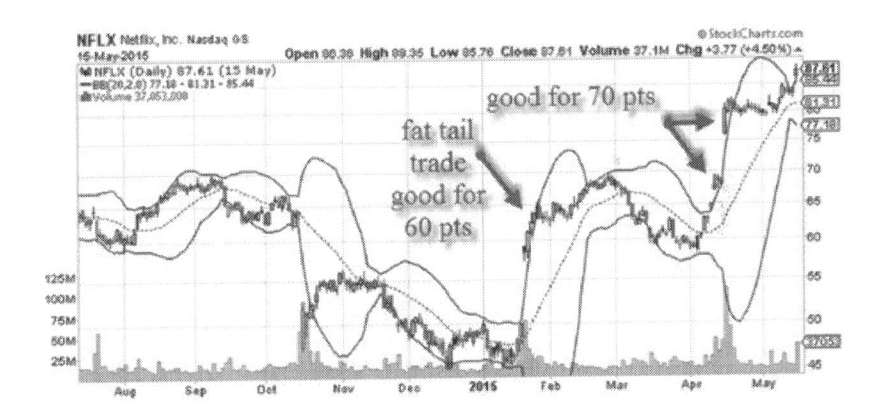

[Chart: NFLX Netflix, Inc. Nasdaq GS, 15-May-2015, annotated "fat tail trade good for 60 pts" and "good for 70 pts"]

Trading a fat tail condition is tricky. It requires some finesse and speed, identification and confirmation. As we see from the Netflix chart above, there were a couple of very profitable fat tail events in 2015.

CHAIKIN ANALYTICS: A SUITE OF MUST-USE TECHNICAL TOOLS

Some of the best and most popular technical tools were created by **Marc Chaikin** a 50-year veteran of markets in just about every capacity. Marc's work refined the analytical tools developed by famed commodities trader and technician Larry Williams (creator of the %R oscillator) and others.

Marc's goal was to get a better feel for price movement under regular market conditions. While creating computerized stock selection models for fund managers, Marc discovered that money flow and accumulation and distribution were key technical elements that complemented price and volume activity.

Today, Marc's name is well recognized around the world of finance for his Chaikin Oscillator and Chaikin Money Flow indicators, both of which are vital tools for technical analysts. Any trader not using them is missing a critical part of his or her analysis.

In the late 2000's, ChaikinAnalytics.com launched to help individual, retail, and institutional investors better tap into changing signals and trends. Marc is a believer that trend analysis provides better profit opportunities than reversals, yet it is extremely important and valuable to know when a trend is turning towards the other direction. The analytics provide a way to see these changes in real time and with amazing accuracy and quickness; a chart sample is below.

TECHNICAL ANALYSTS TO FOLLOW

Carolyn Boroden (www.Fibonacciqueen.com) identifies mathematical and timing patterns based on historical trends and **Fibonacc** numbers (numbers that appear over and over in nature), a common occurrence in financial markets. Her very accurate analysis does not include fundamentals, only statistics that are often so overwhelming it's obvious you need to trade in a particular direction. Carolyn also uses timing mechanisms and symmetry analysis to confirm previous patterns and accuracy.

Alan Farley is simply the best teacher of technical analysis for the swing trader. His website, www.hardrightedge.com, offers a wealth of knowledge for novices and experts. I have used his book, the *Master Swing Trader,* extensively to find some of the most reliable patterns. In fact, it is a book that every technical trader should have in their book library (but finish reading this one first before you start his!).

Alan teaches why price action is key and to look at breakout and breakdown levels for potential. He covers concepts like 7

Bells (specific patterns that should ring loud like an alarm) and patterns like Dip Trip, Coiled Spring, and Power Spike, all of which will give you an edge in determining the next price move.

When I was starting out as an options trading, I told a friend that I really wanted to learn about technicals from a true authority on the subject. He did not hesitate in his answer: "Check out **Dave Landry**." Boy, did he point me in the right direction! I signed up for Dave's email newsletter, and I read all of his books (*Dave Landry on Swing Trading* is the first book I ever owned on technical analysis and, while brief, it immediately got me hooked on the art of technicals).

Dave is a wonderful teacher, because he explains everything clearly and simply. His technical pattern descriptions are legendary. He has identified patterns like Trend Knockout, Bowtie, Micro Double Bottom, and Micro Cup/Handle, and he fully explains chart pattern techniques so you can maximize the opportunity presented by specific price action.

Dave's guidance around risk management and swing trading have made a huge difference to my success as a trader. Like Alan Farley, Dave relies on time-tested patterns to determine trade entry, and he uses disciplined stop-losses to manage risk. The most important lesson I learned from Dave is preparation: You can gain an edge over the rest of the crowd simply by being armed with the best and most up-to-date information at all times.

Todd Gordon (www.tradinganalysis.com) uses Fibonacc numbers in his technical analysis, too, but he also applies the **Elliot Wave Theory** to help him discover points where trends might possibly reverse. This theory is based on historical price action patterns and posits that movements come in waves, usually over five segments (up, down, up, down, up and vice versa). Elliot Wave is not a perfect science. You'll want to mark up a chart with a pencil (keep a good eraser handy) rather than a pen, but Todd is usually quite accurate in pinpointing trend changes using his combined methodology.

Chapter 4 Takeaways

- *Technical analysis is the key to understanding short term market movements.*

- *The market exhibits specific behavior patterns based on fear and greed.*

- *Reliable technical patterns are key to identifying trends and opportunities.*

- *Learn from the technical traders – they'll help you understand the game – and elevate it.*

CHAPTER 5

Turn Down the Noise: How to Manage the Media

> *"In the business world, the rearview mirror is always clearer than the windshield."*
>
> *– Warren Buffett*

Traders and investors are always looking for an edge so they can make more money faster and smarter. When you're just starting out, the first place you might think of looking for tips or clarity in certain situations is the media. The media is actually one of the last places you should go, as they are more concerned with ratings, advertising dollars, and viewer attention than anything else.

The media is notorious for producing too much information, most of which is biased. Biased information is unreliable, and it can lead to cloudy judgment and painful trading losses. Information overload can also cause **analysis paralysis** leaving you completely unable to make a decision and trade.

AT THE END OF THE DAY, YOU MUST COME TO YOUR OWN CONCLUSION AND BASE TRADES ON SOLID ANALYSIS.

With that said, there is no mistaking that investing and trading sentiment follows world events. An airplane that is blown out of the sky with no reason or the death of a highly-regarded government official could cause markets to drop precipitously in the short term (prices will ultimately return to their original level).

And what happens if you hit the panic button and sell everything before you have time to analyze the situation? You'll have to buy your stocks back at higher prices.

Sure, the financial media might offer some great insights into companies, executives and the economy, but by and large, your best bet is to avoid the media noise at all costs, especially when it comes to trading or investing decisions.

You will find that the noise gets louder during a major crisis. For example, Greece's serious economic issues in 2015 served as tinder for the fire that is the markets. The country had severe structural problems and growing mountains of debt for years, but it never had much of a plan to improve their economy or repay their debt. Every year or so, they get backed into a corner, and like clockwork, the Greek government and EuroZone (Greece's biggest creditors) "kick the can" down the road, leaving real solutions for the future

As you might imagine, this kind of uncertainty creates doubt, and investors are not willing to stick around waiting for an explanation. Naturally, the financial media eats this up and creates scenarios of doom that goose ratings. If the media can, they will always put a negative spin on a story. After all, who doesn't love to watch a disaster happen before their very eyes?

Each time one of Greece's debt repayment deadlines approached, world markets would nosedive. Much of that action has been attributed to the media and its distortions of the truth. People would begin to guess at the outcome while investors pulled money out of the markets. Strikingly, markets have roared back to life each and every time! Investors who sell are then forced to buy at higher prices to get back into the game, all the while kicking themselves for not being more patient.

For another example, look no further than 2008. The stock market diving during the out-of-control global financial crisis, and scores of experts were on TV day after day declaring that the market had hit bottom. The message was always the same. "Get in now! This is the bargain of the century! Don't miss your chance!"

This advice was premature (but not completely wrong), because the market had not settled to a place where sellers were finished.

The media wants to keep the upper hand. They will do their utmost to control the story. They will take advantage of the speed and volume of information that is released, which is not always accurate or timely.

For this reason, I urge the traders I work with to ignore the media most of the time. When you do, you will graduate to a new level of trading that is less dependent on emotion and more dependent on the *message* of the market. Only the market itself can clue you into where it is headed. In fact, over the course of my trading career, the media has added little to no value. Instead, I rely on the charts and technicals.

The charts and technicals – not the media – will guide you as you trade. Pay attention to what the markets are telling you and turn off the media noise. You'll be in a much better place.

Chapter 5 Takeaways

- *Do not listen to or trade on what the media is saying.*

- *Focus on the technicals, charts, and market action – they'll tell you what's really going on.*

CHAPTER 6

The Art of Selling

> *The stock market is filled with individuals who know the price of everything, but the value of nothing."*
>
> *– Philip Fisher*

Many traders have trouble selling. However, it is the one act that affords traders the greatest freedom – whether you are booking profits or letting go of a bad position. Why are so many afraid to sell? Here are some reasons:

- I won't pick another winner for a while, if ever again.

- This is my lottery ticket.

- I don't want to make a wrong move.

- I want to hide from a mistake

- Profits aren't big enough – I should wait longer.

- There's plenty of time left.

- I have no idea if I should do something else. Is there a strategy other than selling that will work well in this situation?

Unfortunately, if you're not ready to exit at the appropriate time, you can lose everything you put into that trade. You need to learn how to sell, even if it means booking a small win or taking a loss off the board.

But no matter what, stay true to your system, act on your ideas, and take profits when you have winners. Do not be greedy if you want to stay in the game, and do not be scared of booking a trade.

Yes, people do fear selling – I have heard this numerous times in my travels. But their fear is about more than just selling. They are afraid to sell their golden ticket, thinking that they have to ride it out to the sunset. This is a formula for disaster.

We can discuss every reason to get in or out of a trade, but at the end of the day, you need to listen to what the market is telling you and act accordingly. If you're not taking profits regularly, you'll find yourself wiped out and on the sidelines.

REMEMBER THE NUMBER ONE RULE OF TRADING: TAKE PROFITS.

PS – Nobody will ring a bell telling you when to sell. It is up to you to pull the trigger.

Chapter 6 Takeaways

- *Do not let fear take over*

- *Learn to take profits and lock in gains when you have them*

CHAPTER 7

Save Yourself: The Principles of Risk Management

"Risk comes from not knowing what you're doing."

– Warren Buffett

Have you ever played no-limit hold 'em poker? Then you are familiar with the term "all in," which happens when you place all of your chips into the pot. You either have a winning hand and want the other players to match your bet so you can win big, or you have a losing one and are making a strategic bluff in the hope that the other players fold and you win big, or you are hoping that the next card(s) will complete your hand so – all together now! – you win big.

At its essence, going all in is a very high risk move, because you have no idea what the markets may – or may not – do. This is where risk management comes into play for both the poker player and trader. Some of the best poker players and traders in history demonstrated excellent risk management during their careers, and they have fat bank accounts to prove it.

Never go all in with your capital when trading. This kind of undisciplined risk management will quickly end your career as a trader. Even if you are armed with the best trading system, you will go broke (quickly) without a solid risk management plan. Believe me – I've seen it happen. The need for a short-lived adrenaline rush combined with a fervent belief this one trade is going to hit big has undone many traders. You may get lucky from time to time. There is nothing wrong with but trading on luck is not sustainable.

As a trader, you must have a disciplined risk management approach that ensures:

- You have a diversified portfolio

- You only risk a fraction of your capital on each trade

- You always have cash available for future trading opportunities

Let's look at each of these factors.

A DIVERSIFIED PORTFOLIO

In his book, "*Jim Cramer's Real Money: Sane Investing in an Insane World*" Cramer writes that "diversification is the only free lunch in this whole gosh-darned business. [Stocks] are pieces of paper, and they can go down the drain like toilet paper if they are the wrong ones or if we are in the wrong market."

Harry Markowitz first wrote about the benefits of diversification in the 1950's with an extensive article called

"Portfolio Selection" for the Journal of Finance. In his article, he used mathematics to explain how building a portfolio of unrelated stocks lowers portfolio risk exponentially, eventually down to market risk or even lower (we call this beta risk, which we'll discuss later in the book).

As a trader, your goal is to diversify your portfolio across sectors (energy, financial, technology, biotech, healthcare, etc.), countries, and asset classes, so you can eliminate the risk of holding stocks that always move in tandem. Add some fixed income to counter equities, and add some protection via **index put** as insurance

Take a look at the graph below. The "P" marks the spot where market risk (defined by the capital market line with respect to risk free securities) and return (defined by the efficient frontier line) are optimal. (Note that the number of securities in the portfolio to reach this point on the graph depend on the amount of risk (beta) for each stock.)

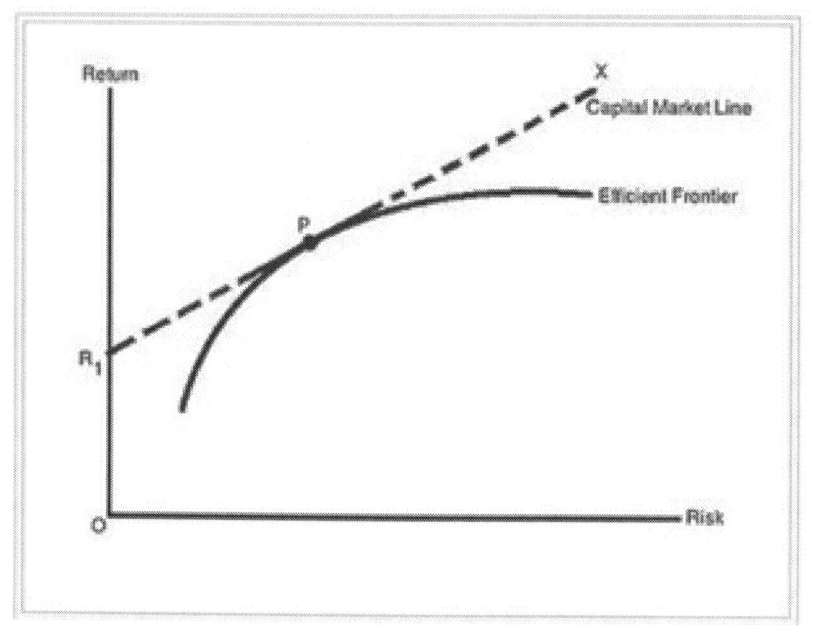

The Combination of Risk-Free Securities with the Efficient Frontier and CML

RISKING YOUR CAPITAL

For stocks, keep your capital risk at a minimum by limiting your positions to 5-7% of your total equity. For a $100,000 portfolio, that means $5-7,000. This kind of discipline ensures you allocate funds in a balanced fashion and adhere to smart risk management rules. Take it one step further and include one or two quality names in each sector (up to the 5-7% total allocation amount). Go another step and cut your losses on a stock purchase at 8%. This means the next trade only needs to earn 8.7% for you to recover that loss.

For options, I suggest dedicating 1.5-2% of your portfolio to this strategy. Because you already have a lot of leverage with options, there is no need to have too much capital at risk.

HOLD CASH

If you invest your entire portfolio at once, you lose the flexibility to jump into new trades. Therefore, your ideal cash balance is 25-30% of your portfolio (we refer to that cash reserve as **dry powder**). New trade ideas pop up all the time, whether it's due to a massive stock selloff, new **PO** or merger news that drives a stock (or entire sector) higher. If you don't reserve cash for future opportunities, you may be forced to sell stocks at exactly the wrong moment. Additionally, holding cash protects you against a rise in market volatility (we covered that in Chapter 4).

Chapter 7 Takeaways

- *Never go all in when investing or trading – always have some dry powder handy*

- *Diversification is the only free lunch – you can cut risk substantially by diversifying through many positions and asset classes*

- *Always keep cash on hand*

CHAPTER 8

Price and Volume: Two Key Technical Elements

> *"Everyone has the brainpower to follow the stock market. If you made it through fifth-grade math, you can do it."*
>
> *– Peter Lynch*

The two most important elements a technician needs to follow are **price** and **volume.** Everything else – indicators, oscillators, momentum readings, moving averages, bands – are secondary. If you only had price and volume to work with, you could be a successful trader. Price and volume are tied together and tend to drive each other.

Let's take a look at why these two tools are so powerful.

PRICE ACTION: THE FOUNDATION OF THE STOCK MARKET

The market is based on price action, so to ignore it is fatal. Every trader and investor votes on price, and voting happens in real time. Higher prices get a thumbs up and lower prices get a thumbs down. Plus, we have historical data to turn to for guidance.

So, how does price action predict the future? That is the million-dollar question! One part of the answer lies in the basic economic principle of supply and demand. When demand is strong (and supply becomes scarce), prices are pushed higher. When demand is weak (and supply increases), prices fall. A stock's price is the point at which a buyer and seller meet and agree to its value. As Warren Buffett once said, "Price is what you pay, value is what you get."

VOLUME: THE FOOTPRINTS LEFT BY BIG MONEY

Volume is the number of shares bought; it shows the commitment from buyers at certain price levels. A higher volume of buying than normal shows very strong interest in a stock.

Volume is important, because it indicates that "big money" is flowing into a stock. Big money is the hedge funds, mutual funds, pension funds, endowments, trusts, banks and other institutions that make up 80% or more of the market's **liquidity** This is the lifeblood of price movement, and once again, it based on the simple economics of supply and demand. A higher supply of stock requires a tick up in volume (demand) to soak up shares and drive the price higher.

Following the footprints left by big money is not easy. First, you need to under- stand timeframe. Big money players are not short-term investors. They understand that to build incredible wealth, they need to hold stocks for the long-term. We're not talking one month, six months, or one year; we are talking about an indefinite amount of time. Some of the greatest investors created wealth by holding stocks over long periods of time, like Warren Buffett, Bill O'Neill, Julian Robertson and Peter Lynch. (In Chapter 1, I said that buying and holding is no longer relevant, and that is still true for the individual investor in the 2 Century.)

Second, volume needs to be carefully analyzed to accurately understand where the smartest minds are putting their money. On the surface, high and low volume levels seem rather simple. High volume means strong commitment by institutional traders at a certain price level, while low volume indicates weak support. That's not the full story, though; there is a bit more analysis involved here. Volume levels also need to be compared with previous time frames. To do this, I will often layer a 30-day moving average across volume bars to see if levels are rising or falling with the price action.

So, if volume is indeed the footprint of big money, do you think that footprints appear all at once? They do not. An institutional investor who wants to take a large position will not buy the full amount in one fell swoop. We often see big money players dive in and scoop up shares on several occasions, using drops in price to build low-cost positions. Hence, you look for several moves by big money in order to put the pieces of the puzzle together.

Let's look at the chart of Arch Coal (ACI) in 2015 to better understand how to follow the big money. The stock had been hammered mercilessly for several years (along with other names in the sector).

During 2015, ACI was on a death spiral, and the acceleration downward really sped up in early May. However, if you look at the chart, you see some volume accumulation during the spring and summer months. By early August, it was near $1 per share. At that point, it was discovered in a filing that famed investor George Soros had taken a large stake in the company.

Once investors knew about Soros' heavy position in ACI, buyers jumped in to accumulate the stock. In just a few short weeks, the stock rallied to over $8, a stunning 700% gain for a stock in a dying sector in just under a month.

SYNTHESIZING PRICE AND VOLUME

While price is always the key to action and volume is always the key to commitment, a combination of the two provides us with the framework to make high probability trades. For instance, a price breakout on higher volume is likely to continue and trend in the direction of the initial move. Stocks tend to follow through on price movements, and heavy volume is a clue that institutional sponsorship is slipping away.

Conversely, a stock that loses altitude after a run higher might pull back some on lower volume, indicating some necessary **back 'n fil** action before taking the next leg higher. We see this in the **cup and handle pattern**. In this pattern, you will see price carve out the right side of a base and either rest or slide a bit lower on lower volume (before resuming upward movement). This movement creates what looks like a handle of a coffee cup, hence the name.

Chapter 8 Takeaways

- *Price action rules over all other activity.*

- *Volume is this big footprint of institutional players.*

- *Used together, price and volume allow you to get your best read on future.*

CHAPTER 9

Option Flow: Follow the Big Money

> *"The professional concerns himself with doing the right thing rather than with making money, knowing that the profit takes care of itself if the other things are attended to."*
>
> – Jesse Livermore

In the previous chapter, I discussed volume as one of the two key indicators that can help guide your trades (the other is price action). You can also use volume, or option flow, to help you understand future action. In fact, you'll often see instances of massive option accumulation just before major news is released (like a merger, sale, or earnings report) and the stock is propelled higher (or lower).

Following option flow is very important – it tells you where the big money is moving. Large funds will often use options as a way to disguise their motives. If they don't want to attract attention, that trader will buy large quantities of options, as it is unlikely to move markets; the same does not hold true for buying a large quantity of stocks.

When you analyze option flow, you will wear the hat of detective. As a detective, you are looking for clues to size, timing and sensibility. Take probabilities into consideration; options volume represents the footprints of a buyer or seller. Ask:

- Does the trade make sense?

- How likely is it that a trader has their eye on a company because news will affect the stock soon?

- Can you piece together a story based on what you know?

Back in 2014, Monster Beverage experienced a very high, very bullish volume of option flow. Coca Cola, which had purchased a big stake in Green Mountain Coffee Roasters earlier that year, was rumored to be interested in Monster, either as an acquisition or large shareholder. Persistent option flow into Coke and Monster, coupled with option strike prices and timing, made perfect sense based on the information I already knew. In August 2014, Monster and Coke struck a deal – Coke would buy a major stake in Monster. Subsequently, Monster stock and options rose sharply higher.

I'd like to point out here that, when compared to stocks, options are ideal leverage vehicles – sometimes giving you 10:1 (or more) leverage from a rise in stock prices. Of course, your timing has to be perfect, since options have an expiration date (stocks don't). As a long-term investor, you can buy an inexpensive stock and hold it for years and years, just waiting for it to increase in value. For an options trader, that move upward has to happen quickly.

As you may have guessed, sizeable option flow typically indicates institutional buying or selling. When option trading volume exceeds about five to seven times normal turnover, my interest is captured. Heavy option order flow means big money is coming into names that are likely to move sharply and quickly higher. Conversely, big money flowing out of names means a sharp decline is coming. My goal is to be on the side of the big money flows as often as possible.

The question becomes: Should I follow the big money? Is one option trade even worth my time? What if it's just a wild bet? You can never know what's going on behind the scenes or what that large option flow volume means. Instead, your goal is to look at the trade with the rational mind of a detective. If you see trading that persists for days or weeks, big money is leaving some very big footprints. Take Monster and Coke. The persistent buying was a great clue that something was going to happen.

Of course, don't forget the charts and technicals. They must also be considered with option flow, especially because flow is not 100% accurate in direction or time. Analyzing the stock chart will help you avoid following option flow that has no rationale behind it. For instance, in March 2015, some very heavy call option buying was seen in Kraft Foods. Kraft is a legendary consumer brand, but it is definitely not considered a growth stock. Hence, options buyers would not normally look for this stock to move higher in the short run – unless there was "something" out there that could move the stock.

When I looked back a couple of years, the stock's movements tended to mirror those of the market. However, when I looked at more recent history, I noticed that there had been several call purchases in February 2015. The purchases averaged in size of

1,000 to 2,000 calls at various strikes above the current price (signaling that higher prices were on the horizon).

At one point, a contract for 20,000 options at a strike just higher than the current price of $62.50 was made (the contract was for Jun 67.5 call strike at .70). Since each option controls 100 shares, the total outlay of capital was $1.4 million (20,000 x 100 x .70). At the time, it seemed like a wild bet. But as is often the case, those who are "in the know" are quiet about their intentions (for good reason!). Note that the chart below shows the adjusted price after the merger with Heinz.

The breakeven level on this trade would have been a stock price of $68.30, or nearly 9.3% above the current price. Historically, Kraft has not moved this much in a three-month time frame except on rare occasions, hence it was enough to consider a trade based on this very heavy flow.

In late March, Warren Buffett's company Berkshire Hathaway announced that it and another fund would pay a substantial premium for Kraft. Eventually they combined Kraft with Heinz, creating a new entity called Kraft Heinz Co. The buyers of those 20,000 KFT June 67.5 calls at .70? They enjoyed an enormous return of over 1,500% for that short period of time.

And this example shows the importance of analyzing option order flow. It is not 100% bullet proof or guaranteed, but it absolutely offers the clues necessary for evaluating a trade opportunity. If the option flow is meaningful, repetitive, and strong, you can follow these big footprints for a winning trade.

Conversely, strong option flow can lead us astray. Sometimes common sense and practicality has to win out. In 2014, with Facebook trading in the low $70's, a buyer purchased 100,000 contracts of the 130 Jun 2015 strike for a nickel. This out-of-the-money trade was a $500,000 bet on much higher prices for Facebook. Now, of course the stock could make a strong move prior to the expiration and gain some value in the option, but the bet was a wild one, especially when you consider Facebook would have had to nearly double in value (and it was already a megacap valuation at more than $150 billion). The contract size was intriguing, but the odds of this bet paying off was less than 2%. It was useless to follow the exact trade, but there was a possibility to find a lower strike that that had a higher probability of success.

Now, why did this trader make this trade? I don't know, but common sense told me it was not a good to follow. In cases like this, the trader is often hedging a position, hence this would likely not be a bet on direction and not worth following.

Chapter 9 Takeaways

- *Option flow represents the stocks that big money is moving into or out of.*

- *Flow is a reliable indicator that a big move may be coming*

- *Technical signals and common sense are critical to deciphering option flow and figuring out whether or not it's good to follow.*

CHAPTER 10

Market Sentiment: Indicators and How to Use Them

> *"The time of maximum pessimism is the best time to buy and the time of maximum optimism is the best time to sell."*
>
> *– John Templeton*

I've already mentioned a few indicators in previous chapters. Now it's time to look at the indicators that signal market sentiment, starting with those that signal market breadth.

Market breadth is an ideal way to gauge the temperature of the market's health at any time. Like most indicators, it provides clues to where price action is likely headed. Market breadth is simply how many stocks are being bought versus being sold and how much volume is behind it. It does not tell you what sector, stock or index people are buying into; rather, it tells you whether money is flowing in or out of the market as a whole.

Coupled with other sentiment tools, such as the put/call ratio, volatility index, rydex ratio and polls, you can get a very accurate idea of what investors and traders are thinking and doing, thus arming you with some powerful predictive readings. Of course, your analysis of these indicators is not always perfect.

Your timing may be off, but sentiment is a valuable tool in your toolbox. Properly reading current market breadth indicators gives you a leg up.

Naturally, there are several different market breadth indicators out there. In general, they provide you with the same information but present that information in slightly different ways. Let's take a look at three of them.

MCCLELLAN OSCILLATOR

The one I use the most is called the McClellan Oscillator, which was developed by Sherman and Marian McClellan in 1969 as a "tool for measuring acceleration in the stock market." At the time, the industry had very few prominent technicians, so the Oscillator was widely adopted.

At its most basic, the tool takes end-of-day data and presents it in cumulative chart form. The data includes an advance/decline line and daily breadth. Taken together and then smoothed using mathematics (10% and 5% exponential moving averages (EMAs) for trend analysis), an oscillator is created. The key, of course, is interpreting the reading to understand where the market may be trending – or to determine if it's reaching the end of a trend (indicated by overbought or oversold conditions).

By itself, the McClellan Oscillator is a great tool, but its summation index, which accumulates all the values, provides an even better reading. It shows you a trend's power, strength, and potential for continuation.

ARMS INDEX (TRIN)

Dick Arms was the first trader to recognize a strong relationship between depth and breadth. He corralled them into a very simple reading called the Arms Index, or TRIN (Traders Index), that uses a ratio of advancers to decliners divided by up or down volume. In general, a reading over one is considered bearish; under one is bullish.

I have found this to be a great contrarian tool at the extremes. Very high readings of around 1.5 indicate the bears are routing the bulls. If the reading lasts 14 days, a powerful rally should ensue soon. A very low reading of .4 means too many bulls are on the bus, and a reversal downward in the markets will soon happen.

CHAIKIN OSCILLATOR

The Chaikin Oscillator, which I mentioned in Chapter 4, interprets the accumulation or distribution of the MACD (moving average convergence/divergence). The oscillator is intense and noisy; it subtracts a 10-day EMA from a 3-day EMA of the accumulation distribution line, and it outlines the momentum implied by the accumulation distribution line. The stronger the reading, the more momentum in price action.

These valuable market breadth indicators can help you determine momentum, trend and strength. While these are very reliable tools, you'll reap the greatest rewards when you use them in conjunction with other sentiment indicators to confirm your analysis.

THE VOLATILITY INDEX (VIX)

The Volatility Index (VIX) shows annualized 30-day volatility and tells us where short-term options players are placing their bets. The VIX rises when fear is present and drops when fear subsides. What causes the VIX to rise? Uncertainty over future events and a high level of complacency among traders and investors. On the flip side, if traders and investors become too greedy, it shows up in a very low VIX reading.

What does this chart mean? It shows that investors and traders are not worried about stocks going down. A contrarian thinker like me might point out that there are no buyers left at this point. With only sellers able to take action, there is little left to boost stock prices (or so the theory goes).

So, when the VIX is elevated and reaches extreme levels, you often have opportunities to buy. The VIX generally moves in the opposite direction of the markets. You could sell volatility or take in high premium with the notion that volatility will surely head back down. When the VIX hits this extreme level, I bracket the daily VIX chart with bollinger bands (a statistical tool; I use two standard deviations from the mean). The bands capture 95%

of the price action in the VIX, but it is the moves toward and through the upper band that tell us when a reversal is about to happen.

The VIX only tells you part of the story, as it provides current, or spot, volatility readings. Looking at future volatility gives you a better idea of the trend and what you might expect on the horizon. The VIX futures term structure prices monthly expectations for future volatility by market players. Hence, each month forward has a value that indicates where market participants expect future volatility to land. Of course, with so much uncertainty, the outcome is often quite different than the current spot VIX (this is the current cash value of the volatility index, as opposed to the future price, which I talk about below). However, you can compare spot and future volatility to gauge the health of sentiment

Typically, future volatility is priced higher than the current spot. Intuitively this makes sense. You would expect to pay a premium for future returns. If futures prices are higher with each forward timeframe, the chart is said to be in "contango." This is a common condition often seen in commodity and bond futures.

PUT/CALL RATIO

Like the VIX, the put/call ratio shows fear among traders. I like to use the put/call ratio as a contrarian indicator. When put volume is high (bets against stocks or the market), this ratio trends higher. When puts reach parity with calls (a ratio of 1 or better), the bets on a lower market are getting heavy.

Why is this the case? Over the long term, the average put/call ratio stands at .61, which means roughly ⅔ of all options being purchased are puts. That is a bullish ratio, which makes sense as the market trend is higher over long periods of time. However, it is in the short term that you see some opportunity to get in on the action.

When total puts/calls hit some very high readings – like a 21 moving average over .90, which is quite rare – the odds increase for a big rally when it turns back down.

Another technician, Larry McMillan, says that when this ratio turns lower and moves under .90, it is a very strong signal that the SPX 500 may move higher by 100 points.

Larry has also identified another condition in which the average peaks and holds for 10 days. Again, the SPX 500 may move higher by 100 points. If you look at the chart below, you can see that the ratio is still rising, so any buy here is far too premature.

CNN FEAR/GREED INDEX

The CNN Fear/Greed Index provides a quick and dirty sampling of investor sentiment based on seven indicators: stock price momentum, stock price strength, stock price breadth, put/call option ratio, junk bond demand, market volatility and safe haven demand. Each indicator is examined to see how far it has drifted from its average level. The results are tabulated and presented in a scale of 0-100. Lower readings indicate high levels of fear, while higher readings represent high levels of greed.

When this aggregate reaches extremes, it is best to use this as a contrarian tool. When the index shows a reading under 20, it means there is extreme fear, which is not often sustainable. The best tactic would be to go long (bullish) on markets. While the timing may not be precise, the bet is that more downside is unlikely to continue.

Conversely, a reading above 80 on the index shows high levels of complacency and too much bullishness. The higher odds play would be to cut positions or short stocks/indices, as this extreme reading is also unsustainable.

INVESTOR POLLS

Investor polls are great sentiment tools as well. I like the American Association of Individual Investors (AAII) polls, which measure the percentage of bearish, bullish and neutral investors. They provide a view of the stock market over the next six months. This data is accumulated weekly. Monumental shifts in sentiment here tell us where money may be flowing.

Keep in mind that polls are coincidence indicators. They show sentiment in the moment and should only be used as secondary sources of information when you're trying to understand the market's next move.

Chapter 10 Takeaways

- *You can measure fear and greed using indicators like the McClellan oscillators, Arms Index, Chaikin oscillator, put/call ratios, and polls*

- *The weight of evidence can mount a good argument for leaning bullish or bearish, but price action is always the final arbiter*

CHAPTER 11

Pricing Options: Implied Versus Historical Volatility

> *"Average investors who try to do a lot of trading will only make their brokers rich."*
>
> *– Michael Jenson*

Understanding how options are priced is difficult, thus making it very easy to miscalculate trades and suffer losses – sometimes very deep losses. An option's value is composed of two things: its intrinsic value and time value (a stock trading below a call option has zero intrinsic value but has time value). In this chapter, we will discuss values based on volatility.

Why do you need to know how to price an option? Simply because you want to pay a fair price for a contract and sell it for a fair price.

Option pricing is not based on some random theory. The Black-Scholes Model (BSM) is an empirical formula that estimates the price of an option over time. This model is used frequently by professional traders and market makers to place a fair value on an option.

One benefit of the BSM is that it has spawned other very efficient option pricing models that are used in derivative pricing and risk management. The model is good at estimating average future volatility, but it is lacking in some crucial areas.

One drawback of the BSM is that it disregards time value, which can only be implied based on supply, demand and time remaining in the life of the option. This is considered by many traders as a gray area of option valuation, but it's something I like to know. I look at historical option pricing to get a good sense of market expectations as it relates to expected, or implied, volatility.

The historical volatility (HV) of an option is simple enough; it's based on the recent or longer term price action of the underlying instrument (stock, commodity, bond or currency). This is considered known volatility, as it's a one standard deviation measure of movement. (Statistics refresher: One standard deviation captures the data points within a data curve 67% of the time within a normal distribution. The other 33% are potential outliers.)

Traders use HV to understand "rate of change." The higher the volatility, the more rapid prices will change. By analyzing actual results and factual data, you can determine how far a stock may go in the future based on the speed it has moved in the past.

To create the volatility measure, you must calculate a standard deviation based on historical price and annualize this figure with the total number of trading days in a year (the square root of 254 is a good number to use). Your answer is the statistical volatility figure for a determined amount of days. This number can be compared to other securities and the market in general. The higher the volatility number, the more likely it is that price will move sharply upward or downward.

Typically, stocks that are in bearish trends will have higher realized volatility readings. This makes sense, as the natural tendency is for stocks to go up. When stocks start moving lower, the price range expands, hence higher volatility.

Let's now look at how to estimate future volatility. Implied volatility (IV) is the expectation of future volatility based on criteria that is not as concrete as historical volatility. IV uses assumptions about demand for the underlying asset and prior movements (but with no certainty). Some believe IV rises when a stock or index is bearish, but that is not always the case. Sometimes IV rises ahead of an earnings report or a regulatory decision (like an FDA ruling that may impact a biotech firm). When the result is unknown, players on both bullish and bearish sides (aka, sellers and buyers) make bets on the outcome. The expectation of sellers and buyers is the main driver of IV.

When you're studying IV, you can use tools to measure how options are priced. First, you can compare IV with historical trends. When IV is higher than the HV, it signals that demand for options is strong and prices are going to rise. This is important, as it tells us more about the expected move rather than the current one. Hence, markets price options in anticipation of moves following certain events.

Below you can see an implied move for Facebook. Earnings were scheduled to be released during the week of November 1, 2015. Notice the expected move (either up or down) of 7.56 points for this series of options, or 7.3% of the current stock price. Of course, there was no guarantee this would happen. In fact, an expected move occurs less than 20% of the time. However, it does give you a point of reference.

It's also noteworthy to point out that the size of Facebook's expected move was much higher than an average expected move of 2.39 points, or 2.3% (seen in the prior week). As you go further out in time, the expected move becomes even larger, rising to 30% of the stock price in January 2017.

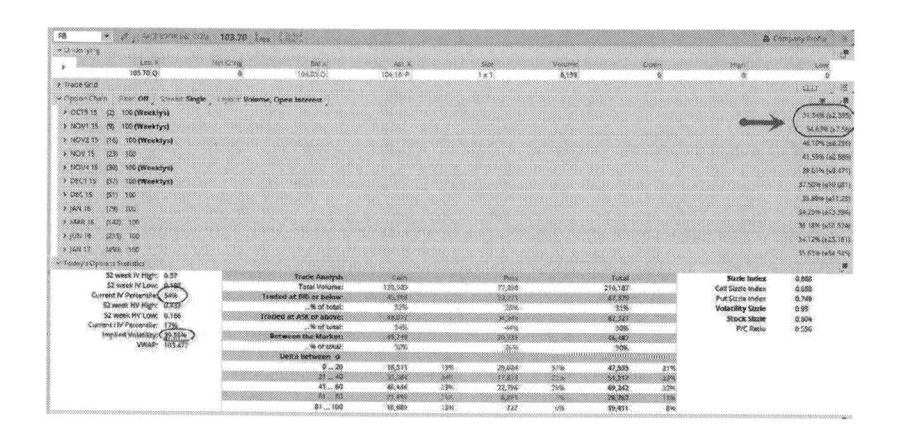

You'll also see an IV number (39.55%) and a comparable HV number (17%) in the chart. You can deduce that current options are priced significantly higher than the norm. However, where does this rank historically versus prior past values? Is it high or ow?

On the TDAmeritrade platform, you can view the current IV percentile. On a scale of 0-100%, Facebook ranks at 54%, aka, its value is 54% higher than past values. In a case like this, selling the premium using a managed-risk strategy would be optimal (more on this and other strategies in a later chapter).

Chapter 11 Takeaways

- *Options are priced based on historical data and implied (expected) moves.*

- *Use IV and HV to help determine option pricing, but don't rely on them as the main driver of trading decisions*

- *Look at pricing from an historical perspective to determine if a trade idea should be considered, but remember it's just one of the many tools you can use in evaluating a trade's potential*

CHAPTER 12

Options 101

> *"The four most dangerous words in investing are: 'This time it's different.'"*
>
> *– John Templeton*

Why trade **options**, you might ask? It's a great question, and the answer might impress you. Options can provide you with income or a safety net. You can use them as leverage or speculation. You can trade them as part of a long-term investment strategy or use them to buy stocks at reduced prices. Or you can analyze them simply for information.

If you understand and trade equity options properly, you can turn a decent stock portfolio return into an exceptional one. But first, you need to understand the basics of options, which we'll cover in this chapter. In Chapter 13, I'll discuss various strategies you can play for different outcomes based on volatility, time and direction. In Chapter 14, I'll show you how to produce income, protect a portfolio via options, and use options to buy into stock at a discounted price.

WHAT ARE OPTIONS?

Options are financial derivative instruments that are contracts between a seller (option writer) and a buyer (option holder). The contract offers the buyer the right, but not the obligation, to purchase the underlying instrument (stock, commodity, index, or bond) at a specific price (called the strike price) by a certain time. When the underlying price crosses above or below the strike price, the option gains intrinsic value

Once the contract deadline passes, the instrument expires and the contract is settled in cash or exchanged for shares under one condition: the option has intrinsic value. Because options eventually expire, time also has inherent value (this is called time decay, which will be discussed later).

There are two types of options. A **cal** option rises when the price of the underlying asset rises, while a **put** option rises when the underlying instrument falls. The terms are related to the action you must take when the option is considered "in the money" by expiration. (There are two distinct styles of options, American and European, which I will discuss later.)

In the stock market, an option gives the buyer or seller the right to control 100 shares of stock without actually purchasing the shares. Hence, an option trader can control a significant amount of stock for a fraction of the price.

Monthly options generally expire at the close of trading on the third Friday of the month. The CBOE recently introduced weekly options, which also expire on a Friday, but unlike monthly options, strike prices are opened each week (or even weeks in advance). In addition, some exchange traded funds (ETF's) expire each quarter (which may not be on a Friday).

WHY SHOULD I TRADE OPTIONS?

Like any investment vehicle, your goal is to use options to increase your stock portfolio returns. As I mentioned above, the leverage options provide is key. You need only risk a relatively small amount of capital to achieve extraordinary gains. Sometimes, you can enjoy 10 to 20 times the rate of return of the underlying security. If you use this leverage wisely, you can enjoy consistent gains.

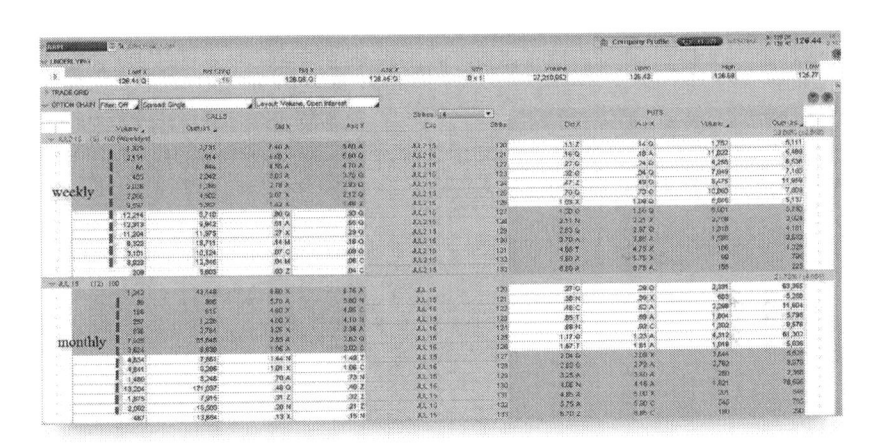

As I mentioned above, there are two styles of options, American and European. The style has nothing to do with the location of where they are traded. Rather, the difference lies in when an option can be exercised or exchanged for the underlying asset. American style options can be exercised at any time leading up to the expiration. European style options can only be exercised at expiration. Most options are American style, but some, like those that underlie futures (such as VIX), are European style.

Moneyness refers to options that are in the money (they have intrinsic value and will be exercised into stock), out of the money (they have no intrinsic value but they do have time value because they have not expired; the further out in time, the more value) or at the money (they have only time value; the option strike hovers near or at the current price of the stock).

At expiration, if a call option is in the money, the underlying stock will be "called away" from the seller, as the buyer will have the right to convert his/her option into stock at the strike price (which could conceivably be lower than the current price).

Conversely the underlying asset will be "put" to the option seller if the put option is in the money. This is because the seller is obligated to take shares if the stock is lower than the put strike (remember, an option seller benefits from the stock going higher).

The buyer of the put has the option to put the shares to the seller in this case. If an option is out of the money by expiration, it will then expire worthless, as there will be no intrinsic value and time will have run out.

Options are often exercised when they are deep in the money with little time decay and a wide spread between the underlying asset and the option. When this happens, the holder of the option can exercise the exchange of options for stock. The seller by contract must release (or accept) the shares on demand.

Options that are at the money or slightly in the money can be exercised but only as the expiration date approaches.

OPTION OBLIGATIONS, COVERED OPTIONS AND NAKED OPTIONS

Because options are a contract between a buyer and seller, the seller is obligated to sell if an option is called or put when it is in the money. Shares or cash must be exchanged at the time. Shares are exchanged if options are written against shares owned (a great way to produce income for a portfolio, but I'll cover this more in-depth in Chapter 14).

For example, if you owned 100 shares of Apple stock (trading at $120 per share) and sold one contract with the strike of $115 expiring in a week, you might be obligated to release 100 shares of stock to the option buyer. But, since you have the stock in your portfolio, the exchange will involve you handing over your shares to the buyer. The difference between the option and the stock will be settled in cash. This is called a **covered call.**

A **naked option** occurs when an option seller does not own the underlying shares and must pay out cash. This is an extremely risky bet and is highly discouraged by brokers, investment managers, and me. A naked option exposes call sellers to potentially unlimited losses (put sellers can stop losses if the underlying asset reaches zero).

While selling options can bring in some nice cash via premium, being unaware of the inherent risks involved can cause severe financial ruin. Some naked option put sellers may intend to enter a stock at a lower price, and while still risky, the intent is understood. I'll talk more about this strategy in Chapter 14.

OPTIONS AT EXPIRATION

When faced with an expiring option that still has value, the owner has a few choices. You could sell the option and take whatever value remains in cash, or you can exercise the option and take the shares. Conversely, the seller can only wait out the clock. Again, we will cover this in Chapter 14.

OPEN INTEREST AND VOLUME

As an options trader, you need to look at data and process it as quickly as possible. Your job is to decipher statistics, patterns and trends, translate this information into a high probability trade, and then make the trade. To that end, the volume and open interest of options tells a story that can help you put the pieces of the puzzle together.

Open interest is the number of **contracts** in existence. However, this is not the number of contracts trades (that is the volume), and it is not a finite number. We often see interest expand when a trader bets that the stock will move very big in one direction or the other. Open interest expands with buyers and sellers of strikes

Open interest also gives us clues about liquidity and the availability of contracts. This is critical information, as a low open interest may not give the option owner much room in which to exit trades easily. Instead, you will be thrown by wide bid/ ask spreads, because there is no secondary market for that particular security. In this scenario, buying or selling can become a major headache. On the flip side, large open interest indicates contracts are being traded and liquidity can be had.

IT'S ALL GREEK TO ME! OR, HOW TO USE THE GREEKS

The **Greeks** are used to evaluate option movement, volatility and time. More specifically, they can help you understand the sensitivity of price movement in options when underlying parameters change. I use several Greeks to gain an edge based on certain criteria: delta, theta, gamma, vega and rho.

DELTA

This measures the rate of change of an option value with respect to changes in the underlying asset's price. The delta is an assigned value (between zero and one) at any point in time. Expressed as a decimal, this is the amount the option will move with a one dollar move in the price of the stock. Delta shows the power of option leverage as the percentage move in the option is much greater than the percentage move in the stock.

For example, a stock trading at $30 with moderate volatility could have an at the money option (the 30 strike call, for instance) with a month to go until expiration selling at 3.20 and a delta of .42. A one dollar move up in the price of the stock (or 3.3%) would be a .42 move up in the price of the option to 3.62 (or 13%). Buying the option gives you nearly 6 times more leverage than buying the stock (13% vs 3.3%).

Let's say Oracle stock is trading at $40.18 a share, and you are looking to buy the $40 call strike in August. The delta is 0.54. The current price of the option is $1.17, so if you bought this call and the stock moved up by one dollar to $41.18, the option (theoretically) would move up $0.54 to $1.71. This represents a 46% increase in the value of the option, whereas the stock would have climbed in value by only 2%.

On the put side, delta is represented as a negative number, but the same concept applies.

THETA

Theta measures the sensitivity of change in the option due to the passage of time (commonly referred to as time decay, since time is constantly working against options). It is expressed in value per year. Divide theta by the number of days in a year, and you arrive at the amount of money per share that the option loses in one day. Theta is negative for long calls and puts, and it's positive for short calls and puts.

Time value decreases as the clock ticks, which explains why the seller usually has an advantage. Time value is basically what is left before the expiration. The other component of an option, intrinsic value, is unaffected by time decay.

Using our example with Oracle on the put side, if we were to sell an at the money put with a $40 strike, theta is -.01. The seller gains a penny each day from time decay.

GAMMA

Gamma measures the rate of change in the delta with respect to changes in the underlying price. Long options have positive gamma, and short options have negative gamma. This relationship exists because gamma rises as the price of the option also rises. The highest gamma pricing occurs with at the money options; value declines as the option moves out of the money or deeper in the money. Using our Oracle example, you can see the $39 and $40 call strikes and the $40 and $41 puts have the highest gamma.

You can use gamma to help neutralize a portfolio. In other words, use other positions to offset risk or perhaps even "delta hedge" (remove risk) so you are less exposed to a loss.

VEGA

Vega measures the risk in changes to implied volatility (the amount of uncertainty over how an option will change in value; it's priced into options). The underlying asset may not change in value, but the implied volatility may change the value of the derivative – in our case the option – substantially. If the market is looking for a big move based on historical analysis, you will see that reflected in vega.

You may take vega positions that anticipate a move or even use vega to hedge a position. In that case, you would become "volatility neutral" so your profits/losses are not exposed to sharp moves in volatility following an event. When you're long volatility, the vega position value is positive. When you're short volatility, the vega position value is negative.

RHO

Rho measures sensitivity to changing interest rate conditions. Interest rate risk affects fixed income investors and traders the most, but option players must also consider the impact of an interest rate change. When interest rates increase, Rho is positive and causes call option values to rise. When interest rates drop, Rho is negative and causes put values to decline. Because interest rate risk is generally higher with a longer time frame, long options have a greater Rho. On the flip side, short options have a lower Rho.

Chapter 12 Takeaways

- *Options trading provides tremendous leverage that stocks and other equities*

- *Open interest and time decay are critical to understanding option values*

- *The Greeks help you understand the sensitivity of price movement in options when underlying parameters change*

CHAPTER 13

Options 201

> *"An investment in knowledge pays the best interest."*
>
> — Benjamin Franklin

Buying a call or put option is a plain vanilla directional bet, but as you get more comfortable trading, you'll want to explore even more ways to play options and reduce your risk. While your payoffs may be lower than a pure directional play, your losses will be greatly minimized. If you want to trade options for income over the long term, you will only succeed by reducing your risk.

In this chapter, we will cover more advanced strategies based on direction, volatility and time. You will notice that I stop placing the dollar sign ($) before put and call prices – this is standard practice in options trading.

DIRECTIONAL BETS VIA VERTICALS SPREADS

A vertical spread is simply buying a call at a specific strike price and then selling it at a higher strike. The quantities purchased (or sold) for each strike price are the same, but for simplicity, we will use the same expiration date. (Different expiration dates can be used. This is called a diagonal covered call, which we'll cover later in the chapter.)

The advantage to buying a spread versus buying a straight option is that you pay less net premium. For example, you could buy a LinkedIn 220 August call, or you could buy a 220/230 call spread. The price of the call is 6.65, while the price of the call spread is much lower at 2.65.

Now, while you did cut your risk by 58% when you bought the spread, you have also limited your upside, or profits, to the size of the spread, which is 10. This means that if the stock exceeds 230 before or by expiration, then we will not enjoy further profits beyond that point. We will sell the option at 230, and the buyer of the 230 call will be able to capture the entire upside.

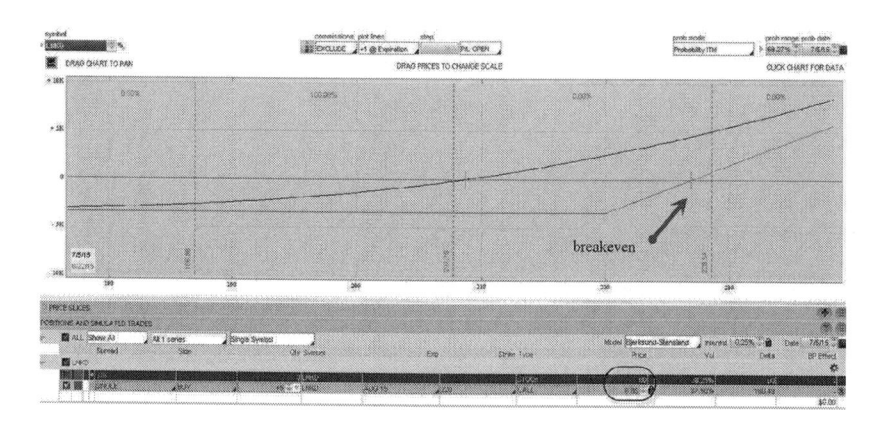

As you can see in the chart, the breakeven point is the cost of the option plus the strike price, or 226.85. The stock must exceed that level by expiration (or earlier) so you can bank a gain on the trade. Gains are unlimited, but we have defined our risk by only being on the hook for the premium paid.

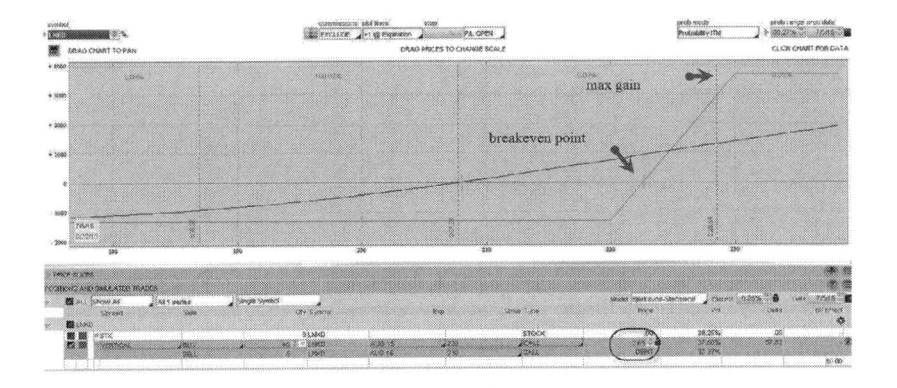

In this example, we see the breakeven is about 58% lower on a straight call (and a 1:1 cost basis). There is a tradeoff, though, as this trade will max out with the stock at 230. It will pay $10, which is still a great return on risk, but we will not participate in profits past the 230 level on the stock. This happens for two reasons: we will owe back any gains on the 230 call (which we are short) but that payback will be offset by gains on the 220 call. Additionally, we have defined our risk by only being responsible for the premium paid, which, as I mentioned above, also reduces our profits.

So, where is the leverage here? It comes in two places.

First, if we were to buy five contracts of the August 220 LinkedIn calls, our cost would be 6.65 x 5 x 100, or $3,325 (that is also the maximum we could lose on this trade). Conversely, if we were to buy the equivalent amount of stock, or 500 shares, we would have to lay out 500 x 207, or $103,500 (207 is the price as I write this chapter).

If the stock is 230 by expiration, the stock owner earns $11,500, or an 11% return – a very nice gain. The call option owner could cash out for $10, a gain of 50% (less the 6.65 cost).

The option gave the owner a 5:1 leveraged advantage over the stock owner. Putting up $3,325, which is about 3.2% of the cost of buying the stock, is a much more attractive proposition. As you can see in the example above, if the timing of the bet pays off, the gain would be bigger.

Second, if you compare the straight call against the long call spread, you can see great leverage here as well. Buying five calls again costs $3,325. However, buying five call spreads at $2.65 each only costs $1,325.

Let's say you choose to apply the exact same defined risk amount on the spread as you would for the straight call. How would that work out? Well, you could buy seven more call spreads for the cost of buying that one call. The beauty of this strategy is that you are not risking more capital but you do stand to make substantially more in returns (up to the $230 stock price). At that level, the spread would max out at $10 and our profit per contract would be $7.35, but 7.35 x 12 x 100 would yield a robust gain of $8,820. That is a spectacular 165% winner, a stunning return on risk.

The straight call would have gained a very solid 50% win as mentioned above. Which would you prefer?

The same principle applies for a vertical spread using put options. Because the buyer would be looking for lower prices, this strategy is comparable to shorting a stock.

VOLATILITY BETS: STRANGLES AND STRADDLES

You can never escape market volatility entirely, but as an option trader, you can take advantage of it. When implied volatility rises higher than historical volatility, it means a very large move is expected, most likely due to a future event. The most common event is an earnings report for the past quarter, which comes along every three months. Prior to earnings, hype and expectation build until a gusher of emotion spills out in stock price action. It's much like a crash off a sugar high – swift and sometimes ugly.

When implied volatility rises, the price of options becomes more expensive relative to what they should be selling for. The historical volatility of the underlying stock provides a roadmap to option valuation. The chart below is a sample of Chipotle Mexican Grill (NYSE: CMG) from July 2015.

In the table, you can see that historical volatility is stable in the 10-20% range, while implied volatility is rising and nearly three times historical. Why? Chipotle's Q2 earnings report was expected just days later, and the market priced in a very large implied move (a combination of the at the money call and put with a 660 strike price). The volatility that's priced in is $49, or roughly 7.42% of the stock price. (Implied volatility for both puts and calls is anywhere from 47-57%, whereas historical volatility is in the 14-17% range.

Option prices are expensive relative to history, so if options are expensive and the market is expecting a big move, you can play for the large move with a volatility play: a strangle or a straddle.

A **strangle** is a bet on a big move (either up or down). The direction of the move is not a concern to the strangle buyer – you just want to see movement. Buying a strangle is a purchase of a call AND a put out of the money. Yes, that's right – you will own both a call and a put. Intuitively you might think, "'How do I make money with this structure?" With this bet, you are playing both sides.

A strangle does not cover all of the price moves, and if there is little movement, there is risk of capturing little to no intrinsic value (known as a gap in the strangle, which is covered by a straddle – more on that later).

Looking to the Chipotle example, a strangle structure for August 7, 2015 expiration might be adding a 670 call at 21.9 and a 652.5 put at 20.5. The purchase of both a call and put would be 21.9 + 20.5, or 42.55 per 100 ($4,255 for each strangle). The breakeven level would be the strike level plus/minus the premium paid, or 712.55 on the call side and 619.95 on the put side.

If the stock moves above 712.55 or below 619.95 the strangle is theoretically in profit mode. (Because time decay has some value, you may see some profits immediately – more on decay in chapter 14.) With an implied move of 49 and historically strong moves post earnings (that exceeded market expectations), this is a bet that may pay off nicely.

KNOW YOUR OPTIONS · 97

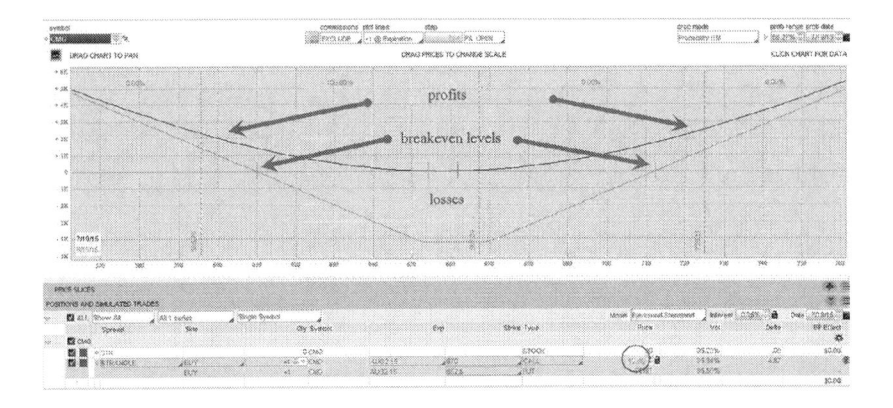

Comparatively, a **straddle** will cover all of the bases when it comes to price. The current price of Chipotle at 660 has a straddle price of 49, and this purchase covers the gap between 670 and 652.50. A straddle is more expensive. You would pay an extra 6.60 (the difference between the straddle and strangle) to cover this gap. Therefore, the breakeven of the straddle is a bit lower – the call breakeven would be 709 while the put breakeven would be 611 (again, because time decay has some value, this would likely be profitable below or above these points).

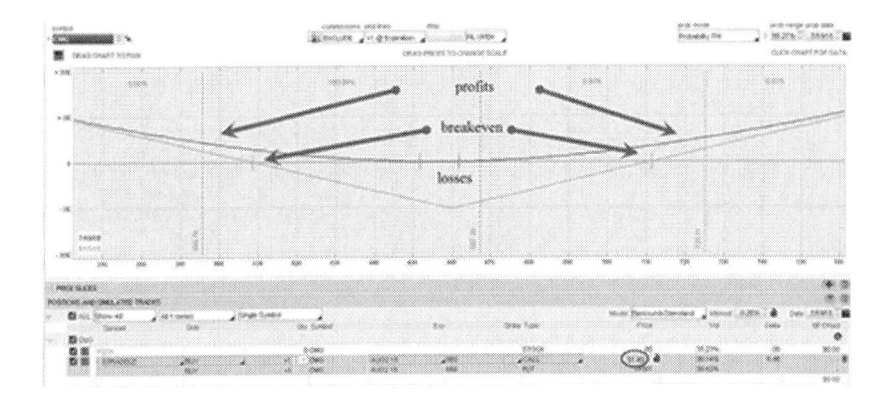

Why buy a straddle versus a strangle? It is really a personal risk preference. The cost difference is negligible, but the strangle offers greater leverage due to the reduced cost. The straddle, on the other hand, could have more value than the strangle after the move is completed and implied volatility declines to more historical levels.

TIME BETS: CALENDAR AND DIAGONAL SPREADS

The flexibility of options allows you to use time as a benefit rather than a hindrance. If you expect moves to happen at certain moments in time, you can use option calendars and diagonal spreads to mitigate risk and play a directional bet – at the same time. Furthermore, you can take advantage of a highly volatile condition to create a low risk bet

I'll use Facebook to illustrate how time can help. Just before earnings, you notice that Facebook implied volatility has risen sharply. This is a normal occurrence, as options are often more expensive before a report is issued due to demand. The stock is currently selling for 96.95 per share. You want to be long a September at-the-money call, as you believe a good move is going to occur by then, but you don't want to expend too much capital. The montage (which shows all of the option strikes and expirations for a specific security) shows the September 1 call costs 6.20 to buy. That is rather expensive; you would need a move to at least 102.6 for a break even. The calendar spread offers a way to get into this trade at a substantial discount, but the scenario has to play out exactly right.

A **calendar** trade consists of buying and selling the same strike option but with different expirations. The idea here is to sell the front month option while going long (buying) the back month. By selling the front month option, you are taking in premium that is less than what you are paying for the back month option, but if the timing works out, then the cost of directional bet is drastically reduced.

For Facebook, you are looking at buying a 96 strike call calendar, selling the July 5 strike and purchasing the Sept 1 strike. You want to sell the July 5 strike, as that will have the maximum amount of premium (earnings will hit just before this option expires). The purchase and sale will be done simultaneously and for the same number of contracts (we'll use the same number of contracts for simplicity, but an unbalanced calendar can be used to optimize a directional bet).

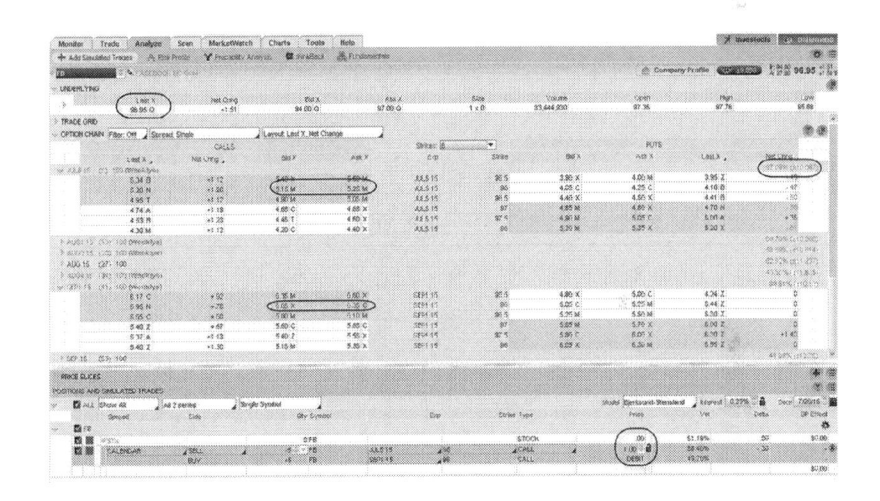

The call calendar currently sells for 1, because the July 5 call sells for roughly 5.20 while the Sept 1 call sells for 6.20. You would be purchasing the combination for $1 and look for Facebook to stay under 96 by expiration, which is two sessions after the earnings release. The expected move post expiration is $10, or roughly 10.3% of the stock price. This is far GREATER than what is normally expected at other times of the year (outside of earnings or other events). If the stock defies market expectations and moves a little or below 96, the July 5 option will expire worthless (remember, you sold this option and hence would like to see it expire worthless).

Should Facebook rise post earnings, your gains would be limited to time decay but would be reduced drastically ONLY if the stock moved past $101. Why is that? You sold the 96 call for 5.20. When added to the strike price, you have the breakeven price of 101.20. Your gains can reduce substantially above 101.20 and can even whittle all the way down to zero.

However, you are long the September 1 call, which carries some time decay along with it. If Facebook falls, you will capture all of the short call (July 5) and still hold the September 1 call. The advantage here is you could essentially be long the 96 Sept 1 call at a cost of 1 rather than 6.20, which is what it would cost for a straight call purchase.

You have cut your risk of being long the Sept 1 call by 83.8%. After the short call (July 5) expires, Facebook is free to go above 96, because the breakeven level is now 97, rather than 102.60.

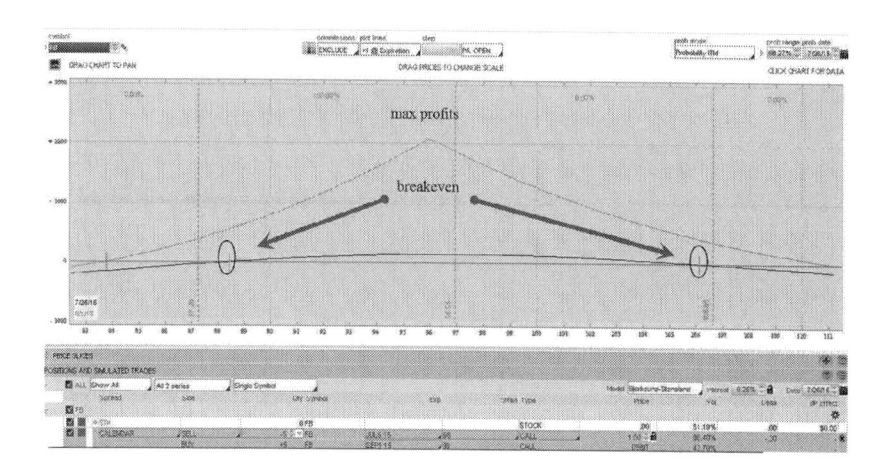

A calendar spread is best utilized when market expectations and implied volatility in the short term are both high, and you have the chance to get on board for a longer dated option at a combined discount. Some call risk is involved, since you are short a call option. If it were in-the-money, the buyer has the right to call the option away. If that happens then the other side of the trade is likely called away to satisfy the obligation (if the quantities are the same, no further obligation, aka, additional funds, is necessary).

DIAGONAL CALENDAR SPREADS

A **diagonal** is similar to a calendar spread, only you use different strike prices when selling premium. A diagonal is often used as a way to capture premium against a longer dated position. You would cut the risk of the long position by strategically selling a call or put without exercising or converting it.

One tactic I often use involves buying a long call or put out of the money position. I collect the premium by selling shorter-dated options to cover the cost of the long position. That might sound confusing at first, but it's worth learning, as it's really one of the best overall options strategies.

Let's use Tesla (Nasdaq: TSLA) as an example. You believe, based on your technical and fundamental analysis, that Tesla will outperform earnings expectations and rise significantly higher in the coming months. This stock sports a high **multiple** and a rich **valuation**. Its growth metrics are strong, and until that changes, the stock continues to attract buyers. The current stock price is $266 per share, and based on your calculations, TSLA could be well above $300 in eight months.

Since it is Aug 2015, buying the 300 Mar 2016 strike would cost a bit more than $20 per contract, or $2,000. That is a bit steep, as this bet is made with so many uncertainties over a long timeframe. You will implement a diagonal strategy to help you cut risk by at least one third.

You will buy three March 2016 TSLA 300 strike calls at 20.95 each. Your total purchase will be $6,285. Next, you will target a lower strike to sell three calls against. Your objective is to find a strike that has some nice premium to capture but will allow you some wiggle room, as you do not want this to be in the money quickly. If it does, you still want to make an overall profit if you do get called away.

The Sept 2015 285 strike is selling for about 8.05, which is about 38% of the Mar 300 call strike you just purchased. If you sell three of these calls, your account will be credited $2,415 immediately. You have just cut your risk by more than 38%. **The absolute worst outcome now is that you could lose 62% of your Mar 2016 300 call purchase, or $3,870.**

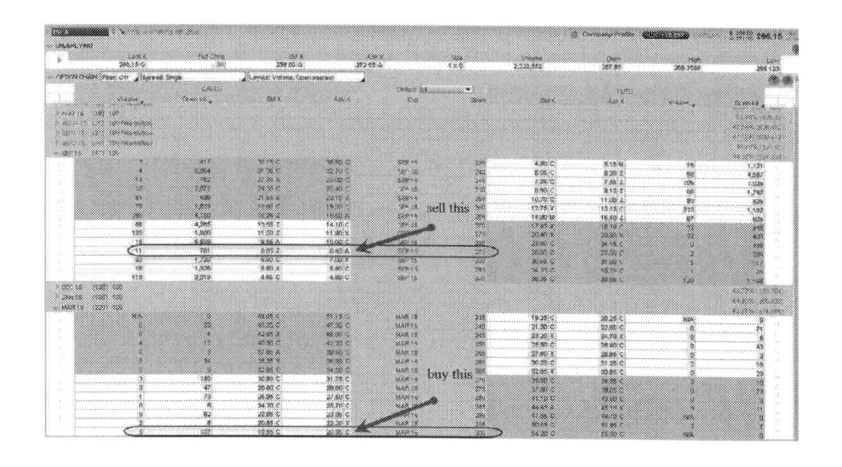

With the stock well below the short call strike of 280, it's now a matter of waiting it out until the September expiration. At that time, if TSLA is under 280, the call you sold will expire worthless and you would still own the March 2016 300 strike call. You could sell another call against your long call (like the Dec or Jan strikes), perhaps collect another 8, and further reduce the cost of your long call.

If you're fortunate with timing, you will capture all of the premium for the long March call before the stock starts to move higher. And if you repeat the exercise with the short calls two more times, you could conceivably recapture your entire $6,285 paid for the Mar 2016 300 strike call. That means you would have a "free ride." You'd have nothing to lose and everything to gain! If the stock suddenly surges past the 300 strike prior to the Mar 2016 expiration, then you could be looking at a highly profitable gain.

Now, of course your timing has to be just right for this to work out exactly as planned, and since the future is uncertain, there are many scenarios that can disrupt your plans. The stock could run too early, moving right through your short strike. If that happens, your long call would offset your short call (as long as the quantities were equal), and any difference would be settled in cash. Since the long Mar 2016 300 strike has more time decay, it would likely have more value, and you could earn a small profit. At that point, the trade would be closed (but you could re-open it).

If the stock fell hard in the short term, your long Mar 2016 call could also lose value, but by selling a short call you are somewhat insulated by the decay factor. The short call (which you sold for premium) would benefit you, as it will decay at a much faster rate. While this could start out as a losing trade, you have to remember that the time remaining on the long call is to your benefit.

Time strategies have some great profit potential if all the pieces fall into place. Calendars and diagonals offer a great chance to participate in options trading. Both strategies cut risk substantially against a directional bet if the underlying stock has a period of sideways movement or if **implied volatility** is much higher than **historical volatility** (these terms were covered extensively in the previous chapter).

Chapter 13 Takeaways

- *Different structures allow you to participate in a trade while significantly cutting risk.*

- *Vertical spreads are directional bets up or down, but they limit the amount of your gain based on the size of the spread.*

- *Straddles and strangles are volatility bets that take advantage of outsized moves in the stock price.*

- *Calendars and diagonals are time bets that give you an advantage if a move happens later rather than sooner.*

CHAPTER 14

Options 301

> *"It never was my thinking that made big money for me. It was always my sitting. Got that? My sitting tight!"*
>
> *— Jesse Livermore*

Many investors prefer to create a portfolio that includes dividend-paying stocks (stock that divvy up and distribute profits among shareholders). During challenging market conditions, a nice yield (cash dividend/price) provides income, portfolio protection, and even some shelter from losses, depending on the stock. It's a smart strategy for those who are risk averse and prefer to hang onto their capital.

What if I told you that some options strategies could provide you with some extra income, allow you to purchase a hot stock at a discount, or even protect your investment entirely? And it only costs a small amount of capital? I probably have your attention now!

In this chapter, we will delve into the world of **selling option premium** This clever strategy requires a full understanding of options rules. Do your homework, and it can become a winning technique if well-timed and properly executed.

As you know, an option transaction requires a market – a buyer and a seller. The option buyer is only required to pay the premium stated for a particular strike at a specific expiration. This is called defined risk, aka, the maximum loss is what the buyer paid for the option. The seller on the other side of the trade takes the premium and the risk of being called or put stock if the option goes in the money, where the option can (and usually will be) exercised.

An option seller is always looking for the option to expire or decay close to zero. Your goal is to collect premium from the buyer on the other side of the trade. Options are a zero-sum game. One side will win and the other side will lose. While an option value includes both intrinsic (if in the money) and time value, the decay always works in favor of the seller. (In Chapter 12, we talked about how theta decay builds portfolio value on a daily basis.)

So, if you are not interested in buying a call, you are taking a bullish stance. Taking the other side requires a bearish one. Because of time decay, the underlying stock does not necessarily have to move down, as you would expect from a bearish trade. Selling premium **at the money or out of the money** could be a winner if the stock just goes sideways. A strong relationship exists between option premium and time – it's called volatility (implied and historical volatility are discussed in Chapter 11).

Selling calls involves some patience. Since time is the friend of the seller, intuitively it makes sense to ride out a sale as long as possible. Yet, selling options without some protection in place, like buying another higher (or lower) strike, is quite risky and is called **selling naked options**.

KNOW YOUR OPTIONS · 107

If you are under-capitalized (or simply have a small account), you would not be allowed to sell naked options. Those who have plenty of capital to work with can sell naked options, but they face major risks. This strategy does NOT define your risk, and while capturing the option premium is high and quite attractive, your account can swiftly be taken out in a body bag with an adverse move. Why? Because selling calls naked has unlimited downside risk! In theory, a stock could rise forever – and being on the hook for the upside could be devastating. If selling calls, always have them covered by an equivalent amount of shares.

Here's a simple example of selling option premium: Call option for Gilead Sciences (Nasdaq: GILD) seem to be quite high. In fact, call prices are close to the all-time high. However, the current market environment seems shaky, so even though the stock is up strongly for the year, further upside seems limited. With the stock at 117.86, you look at the 120 calls that expire in three weeks (Aug 2015). This strike has strong open interest and has been active (trading) recently. Liquidity is good at this strike, so getting in and out should not be a problem.

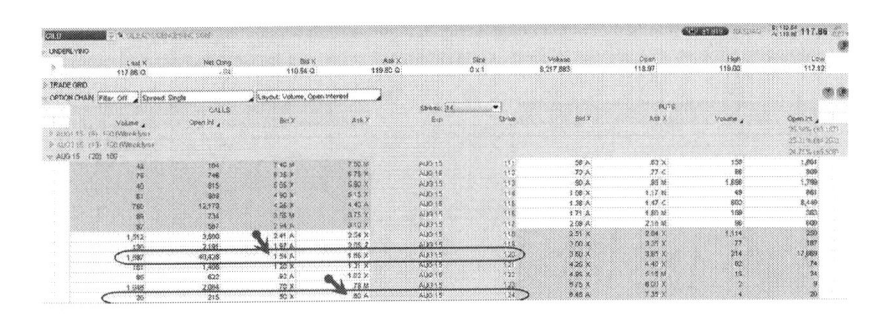

As you can see from the option montage, the strike you are targeting has a bid/ask spread of 1.54 x 1.66. This means (in theory) that the option could be sold at 1.54 (bid) or bought at 1.66 (ask). The 8 cent spread is the middleman's "fee". (Note that prices can be offered, or bid, inside the spread, but the shown bid/ask is what the market is offering at a particular time.) With this trade, you would be targeting the bid side, or 1.54. This is where sellers reside.

Your ideal trade would sell Aug 120 strikes. Because you want to define your risk you would buy a higher strike to create a spread; the 124 call seems good here. You would attempt to work the order at $1 for the call spread. This would be a credit, hence your cash balance would increase by the total contracts times the spread price. If your goal is to make $500 on this trade, you would sell five contracts at $1 each (5 x 1 x 100 = 500). Your risk is defined as the difference in the spread less the premium you collected, or 4 - 1 = $3 per contract. (124 - 120 = 4. You collected 1 so your risk is 3 if the stock moves out past 124 by expiration.)

With the stock currently below the short strike (Aug 120 call), you have a bit of cushion – but not much. With three weeks to go on this trade, you would like to have Gilead stay under 120 by the expiration. You actually have more cushion than meets the eye, as your profit zone for the entire trade is all the way up to 121. Why is that? Remember the $1 we collected by selling the spread? Add that to the short strike, because it's already "in the bank." Your true breakeven level is 121. You start losing money above 121 but losses are capped at 124. Beyond that level, you no longer have any risk as long as you keep the trade in place.

There are only two outcomes for this strategy – profit or loss – but the degree is different and based on time of closing. For a maximum gain, the seller of the call spread would hold it until the expiration, letting both sides (short and long call) expire worthless. The seller would then keep all of the premium collected. No further action is necessary.

This can be risky, though! Trying to hold out for every drop of profit can turn into a disaster in no time. A good rule of thumb is to close out a trade once 80% of the premium has been removed (hence, selling the call spread at $1 could be bought back at $0.20 – an ideal move).

I need to mention one important element to selling premium, and that is a margin requirement. A brokerage is not going to share risk with the premium seller. It requires the client to post margin in exchange for creating this type of structure. The difference between the premium collected and what the seller is on the hook for is posted, and cash is held until the trade is closed out entirely (some accounts are ineligible to sell premium due to the inherent risk involved).

How does this trade work out on a risk/return basis? This trade expires in about three weeks. Collecting $1 is about 0.8% of the price of the stock ($117.86). If you keep the entire credit, you can annualize this return to be roughly 13.8% ($1 x .008 x (52 weeks / 3 weeks). Of course, this is not the absolute return, but it can be used to compare annualized returns versus other trading strategies.

BUYING A STOCK AT A DISCOUNT

Let's say you have your eye on buying some shares of Intel (Nasdaq: INTC). You see the stock is currently selling at 28.96, but you would like to get in at a lower price – around 28. You have the cash available to buy 500 shares of stock. Do you wait for the stock to fall less than one dollar, or do you take a proactive approach? The latter requires options (and it's a nice way to get paid, you just need to wait for the "fat pitch" before swinging for the fences).

Since you would consider buying 500 shares today, let's instead sell five Sept 29 puts for $1. By doing this, your account would receive immediate credit for $500 (1 x 5 x 100 per option). Your risk here is simple. If the stock is under $29 by the September expiration, you will have 500 shares "put" to you (which is what you want). But wait a minute! You want to buy the shares at $28, right? Remember the $1 credit per contract you received? You'll keep that, thank you very much – and that will reduce the cost of purchasing the shares of Intel stock by $1. Your net cost is $28.

Now, there is always a "what if" in every scenario. In this case, the "what if" is a potentially good result. Let's say Intel goes higher through the short strike of $29, and the stock is not put to the option seller. Since the stock price is out of the money (and assuming that is the case through expiration), then the seller keeps the $500 credit, and you can write (sell) the put one more time and collect more premium.

For the Sept strike risk/reward analysis, seven weeks remain in the life of the put. The $1 is about 3.4% of the price of Intel. Annualized, you see this is a robust 25% return ($1 x .034 x (52 weeks / 7 weeks). However, you still do not own Intel yet, but given the fact that their dividend yield is currently 3.4%, the short put strategy is far superior. In addition, this strategy can be used until the shares are finally put.

WRITING COVERED CALLS

To go one step further, assume the shares are put to the seller at $29 per share. You are now the proud owner of the stock at a cost of $28 per share (remember, the premium collected reduced the cost of shares). You are entitled to be paid the dividend, a solid 3.4% annual return. You could also sell calls against your shares now, collecting more premium (which acts like another dividend).

Here's how this works: It is now October, and you hold the 500 Intel shares that were put to you last month. The stock is currently at $29, and it appears Intel may have some upside based on your chart analysis, but it may not be much more than 7% over the next couple of months. You see the Jan 2016 31 call strike could be sold for $0.86 cents per contract x 100. You can sell five of these contracts, collect an addition $430 of premium, wait for the January expiration. You will be covered with your 500 shares in case the stock moves through the strike price and the shares are called away. This is a **covered call** write

Would that be a horrible event? On the "money side," not really. If the stock is called away, it means the stock is through $31. Your cost at $28 makes this a 10.7% winner. But, if you add in the premium collected from selling the 31 call strike, your total return increases to 13.7%. The only downside is you would no longer own the shares. (And now you owe taxes. Ever hear the saying, "If you have a tax problem you probably had a good year?" It's true.) However, you can repurchase the shares again in the open market, and run this drill all over again.

Should the stock not exceed $31 by January expiration, the call would expire worthless, you would keep the premium collected, and of course you could write those calls one more time.

PROTECT YOUR INVESTMENT

You have many ways to protect your investment and guard against future events that can trigger a nasty selloff. One of the simplest and cleanest ways to protect your portfolio is to purchase put protection via index options **Exchange Traded Funds,** or ETF's, are an ideal tool for buying short or long term protection. The four main index funds I suggest are the SPYders (spx 500 proxy), DIAmonds (Dow Industrials proxy), IWM (Russell 2K proxy), and the QQQ (Nasdaq 100 proxy). Each of these instruments are widely followed, actively traded, and excellent at providing good liquidity in option open interest.

Where many traders fail in managing risk is underestimating the ability of markets to correct and move lower sharply. Investors are often far too **complacent** and end up chasing after protection rather than being proactive.

For example, if you had a portfolio of stocks highly **correlated** to the SPX 500, then you might consider buying some SPYder puts as insurance, especially if you believed a market downturn was around the corner. Frankly, attempting to time a downturn is foolhardy but portfolio protection is not. While it may drag overall portfolio performance, protection is certainly nice to have during those moments of sheer market terror.

Buying some index puts to protect a portfolio is far less expensive than shorting an index, and it defines your risk. The nature and timing of the put buys can be arbitrary, but if you stick with a plan to always have some protection, then market surprises will bother you less.

On the flip side, call spreads could be sold to create some income, and you could sell the premium on indices as a way to protect a portfolio. Any of the indices are eligible for such a strategy.

You can also protect individual stocks by doing what is known as a **collar** This is an easy way to limit downside risk using options. Let's say you own Netflix stock (Nasdaq: NFLX). The stock is up strong for the year, and you do not want to lose any of those gains. If you own 300 shares of stock, you can collar this by selling three calls AND buying some puts at the same time. You do not want to completely stifle the upside potential, as it appears Netflix can move up a bit more. You collar the stock to give it some room to run higher, but if it does fall, you have some downside protection.

Collaring a stock can be rather inexpensive and perhaps even a no-cost transaction. Imagine buying some insurance against the market moving down for pennies on the dollar or even for free. Maybe you'll even get paid to do it.

In the Netflix example, the stock is at 114.31. The all-time high is around 119, but you think it has downside potential to 105. The October monthly option offers good premium on both calls and puts. You could sell three Oct 125 call for $5, use that money to buy three Oct 105 put for $5, and the cost would be zero. Owning the shares has you covered on the short Oct 125 calls, so in case that is called away, you do not have to post more cash than is required by the margin.

How does this collar work in your favor? Simply put, if the stock falls, you have protection with your long put against high volatility and a sharp market decline, which could take the stock well toward the strike or even lower. Further, the short call would decay and offset some losses of a stock decline. Should the stock move higher, and perhaps even through the short strike (Oct 125 call), you could have your stock called away at 10+ points higher (and enjoy a nice profit). The upside would likely be lost above 125, but you could make adjustments if needed.

To sum up, selling premium can create income, allow you to buy a stock at a lower price, and protect a portfolio.

Chapter 14 Takeaways

- *Selling premium is a great strategy for generating income.*

- *By selling puts, you can also buy into a stock at a lower price.*

- *By collaring a stock, you can obtain cheap protection around a stock simply by selling a call and buying a put.*

- *A covered call is a plain vanilla strategy but a nice way to generate income against a stock holding.*

CHAPTER 15

Listen to and Learn from the Pros

Experience is the greatest teacher of all. We can learn from each other's successes and failures, which is why I have included stories from trading pros in this book.

The one common bond between these traders is their willingness to teach others. Knowledge is power, and there is nothing more powerful than learning from the best. Enjoy – and learn from their trials and tribulations.

STEVEN BURNS

If I looked up the definition for discipline in the dictionary, I would find a picture of Steve Burns. Though young, he has mastered the craft of options trading. He boasts a stellar track record, but what I truly admire about Steve is his control, rules and structure. He constantly talks about risk management, stop losses, and when he will get out before even putting on a trade. Steve's ability to control risk has allowed him to take "chance" out of his game. Oh sure, the occasional surprises come along, but Steve controls his emotions by employing strict rules – and actually following them! I'm pleased to offer some valuable thoughts from Steve Burns below. You can find more from Steve www.newtraderU.com, including several of his publications. His Twitter handle is @sjosephburns

WHAT IS A TRADER?

Traders are often misunderstood. While investors are more mainstream, traders are viewed as risk takers or having ulterior motives. There are some significant differences between investors and traders, but the notion that serious and profitable traders are gamblers is far from the truth.

Investors grow their capital by investing in a company's stock. Traders increase their capital by trading a stock's price action. Some traders may be undisciplined or inexperienced enough to be perceived as gamblers, but the most profitable traders are entrepreneurs operating a business. Gamblers risk money when the odds are not in their favor, but good traders only take risks when the odds are on their side.

Likewise, the differences between gamblers and traders are mirrored by the disparities between gamblers and casinos. Casinos take bets from gamblers that have the odds in their favor over the long term and set table limits to manage their risk exposure. A profitable trader resembles the casino more than a gambler because they always keep the odds in their favor, play the long game, and manage their risk.

Profitable traders should be viewed as entrepreneurs that take calculated risks for the opportunity to make profits. Most businesses buy and sell products based on supply and demand; they buy wholesale and sell at retail to earn a profit. A trader makes money by buying low and selling high or buying high and selling higher. It is always based on supply and demand. Most experienced traders find success during a market trend, just like a business will profit by finding and selling the hottest merchandise.

The greatest opportunity when it comes to trading is also the biggest danger. Unlike other professional fields, there is a low barrier for entry. It's easy to open up an account and start trading alongside seasoned professionals. You can't practice law or medicine without spending years of study and gaining practical experience. Trading and investing is no different. It is all too easy for a new trader to enter the market unprepared and quickly lose their trading capital.

The prepared trader will reap the benefit of their less educated adversary. A trader's profitability comes from being on the right side of the market when it makes a move. When you are on the right side, money goes into your account, and when you are on the wrong side, money leaves your account. A trader's education process involves learning how to be on the right side of the market the majority of the time. Profitability comes from maximizing your time in winning trades and minimizing the amount of time in losing trades. Focus on making large profits when right, and strive to lose a small amount of money when you're wrong. That is the key to profitable trading.

Another important element of a trader's education is to understand the importance of risk management. Most traders struggle because they trade too big and take on too much risk. Trading is as stressful as we make it. One single trade should never carry the threat of a large emotional or monetary loss. Each trade should only be one of the next one hundred trades. This is accomplished by trading enough capital that you can handle losing, while risking enough to make the trade worthwhile. One way of accomplishing this is through asymmetric trading vehicles like options. Options allow a trader to risk a little for the possibility of making a lot. These contracts allow traders to define their risk and limit their losses while keeping the upside potential unlimited until expiration. Options are an important tool in a trader's toolbox.

While investors look at the current value of a company versus the future potential for price appreciation, traders analyze the future potential of trending prices based on the current supply and demand of the stock. Higher highs and higher lows day after day on the daily chart tell a trader that a stock is in an uptrend. If a stock is unable to get through an overhanging price level on the chart, that tells traders that there are no buyers at that price level and the stock has hit resistance. Volume on a chart is a voting system; the higher the volume, the better the odds that the price will stay at the new levels and continue to trend. Try to go in the direction of least resistance with a trend until it becomes extended from short term moving averages or its price becomes too volatile. This is where the trend can bend. Always look for the easy money by going with the flow as long as possible.

Trading can be an enjoyable and profitable way to spend your time if you trade in your comfort zone. It can also be a nightmare if you risk too much and trade too often. Remember that the only reason to trade is to make money. I love trading but I hate losing money.

I have had some great experiences over the last 20 years. Like most, I benefitted from the dot com boom and had enough money in my account to pay off my first home in March 2000. That was an amazing feeling at age 28, and it hooked me for life. There are a lot of business opportunities out there, but it's hard to envision them having a better upside than trading. Professional trading has a low entry cost and offers great profit potential with minimum risk in an environment that you control 100%. Best of all, there are no employees, no leases, and no boss.

My many years of learning things the hard way led me to start NewTraderU.com as a way to help and inspire new traders. I blog, publish books and create e-Courses on the dynamics of trading psychology, risk management, and trading methodologies. They are designed to give new traders a shortcut to profitability by sharing what I wish I had known twenty years ago.

TIM MELVIN

I have never met Tim Melvin personally (as of this writing) but after many conversations with him over the years, I feel like I know him very well. Tim is a lifelong market player, author, and baseball enthusiast who demonstrates the art of patience. A tried-and-true value investor, Tim looks for the best ideas money can buy but not necessarily the most expensive. His investments might take many years to pay off for him, but value players are not looking for the quick hit. He represents an investor from a different era when buy and hold was rewarded, and his record of success is compelling. I'm sure you will find him and his story below fascinating and humorous. You can find more from Tim at marketfy.com, where he is the author of the Deep Value Letter.

THE AWAKENING

I am always shocked when Bob asks me to participate in one of his projects. There could not be two people more different than Bob and I. He is a trader with short time frames. I still have stocks from 2003 in my portfolio. He buys options In the few cases that I use options, I sell them to create positions. I focus on corporate valuation I am not always sure that, like many traders I have met, Bob knows what business his targets are in. He roots for mega payroll baseball teams and likes ice dancing with stocks. I root for old school blue collar baseball teams that use skill and baseball savvy to win games, and I think hockey is just soccer with sticks. We are not very much alike but we are good friends, and the financial markets have been good to both of us over the years.

I have tried that whole trading thing. It is just not for me. I recall my very first futures trade. It was back in 1989, and I was with Dean Witter out in Modesto, California. I was in my office one day when I saw a group of older brokers gathering in one guy's office. They were all quite excited about some chart. I asked what the big deal was, and they patiently explained to me, the new guy who never went to college, that this spread tracked the relationship between municipal bonds to treasury bonds. Municipal bonds (munis) had never traded above a certain level on the chart, and prices were now back to that upper level. All you had to do was sell muni contracts and a corresponding number of treasury bond futures per spread, and when the spread inevitably corrected itself, you could make thousands of dollars per contract. The spread margin was just $250 per spread as I recall, so this was going to guarantee some big, big money.

These guys were all MBAs, and I was barely high school educated, so I figured they knew what they were doing. I put on as many spreads as I could afford, and I put all of my clients in the deal. The next morning, the spread had not blown through that never-before-reached level. Instead, it just kept going the wrong way. I spent the next few days not answering my phone, hiding from the margin clerk, and trying to puke as little as possible. It was my first experience with the guaranteed-to-work trades. They never do, of course, but you can only learn that lesson the hard way.

I had other forays into trading over the years with mixed results but it doesn't really fit my personality very well. I do not want to put off my afternoon nap because the markets are still open. I have no interest at all in getting up twice a night to check Forex moves like some of my currency trader friends. I do not want to spend all day glued to the screen watching prices tick by. Nothing about trading interests me.

With the help of a mentor, I discovered value investing. With the help of an old fella in my office in the early 1990s, who favored golf and drinking over working (I am not much on golf myself), I discovered community bank stocks. These stocks are a magical combination. They are capable of turning out very high returns over time, but they are also very illiquid, and that scares most individuals away. However, the rules of the game are fairly simple, and the larger funds and ETFs cannot trade in the space. Increasingly, community bank stocks are becoming my own personal playground. You don't need to be glued to the screen, skip a walk with the dog during market hours, or miss an afternoon nap because the market is open. When you are focusing on value, especially illiquid value like community banks, day-to-day does not matter. Month-to-month hardly matters. That fits my personality to a T. I buy cheap and hold.

This is not to say that I am not busy during the day. I research and study almost constantly. I read filings on interesting companies. I relentlessly track what successful investors are doing with their money and re-engineer their methodology. I run hundreds of tests on various theories to discover what does, and most importantly, what does not work in the market. The financial markets are the most interesting and rewarding intellectual puzzle of all time, and I really enjoy the effort. I get up each day excited about what new piece of the puzzle or great idea I may uncover.

Lately I have been doing a lot of work on combining deeply undervalued stocks with momentum filters, and the results are very promising. By applying momentum filters, it appears that we can magnify returns and reduce drawdowns. I am fascinated that by combining two approaches that seem to be polar opposites, we may well be able to improve long term returns. Stuff like this makes the day interesting to a geek like me

One of the questions Bob bought up when we talked about his project was what the stock markets had taught me about life. The lessons are endless. There will be winners and losers. Nothing ever stays the same forever. Like it or not, in every transaction, the other side is looking to take advantage of you. In the short term, survival is just as, if not more so, important as victory. If you are buying, have a strong idea why the guy on the other side is selling. Reverse this if you are selling. Your emotions are your worst enemy. The easy money never is. Stick with probabilities but be aware of gambler's ruin. Just because you have a high probability trade or investment does not mean you cannot have a very long string of adverse outcomes. Patience pays. If you do what everyone else does, you will get what everyone else gets. On balance most people are crazy.

The hardest thing to do as an investor is deal with the bad times. No strategy works all the time. Bear markets happen, and they can hurt. As a value investor, I have to be prepared to underperform a significant period of time and not abandon my strategy. It takes a great deal of discipline and conviction to stick to the plan. I have trader friends who have successful methodologies, but when their approach is temporarily out of step with the market, weeks and months go by without a good trade.

It is very easy to walk away in disgust and frustration. The only way to gain confidence and discipline is to always be learning, testing, exploring and refining your approach to the markets. Conditions change, and what worked yesterday may not work tomorrow. An out-of-the-box static system may work for a brief period of time, but it will fail eventually – often with spectacular consequences.

I am often accused of being anti-trading, because I rant and rail against short term trading. It is not that I am against trading. I have many friends that are traders, but you need to be aware of something. Successful trading is a lot like baseball. Approximately 450,000 kids play high school baseball each year. Most dream about pitching game seven in the World Series, hitting mammoth home runs, and playing center field for the New York Yankees. About 25,000 of those kids will be able to play in college. Many of them get a free education out of the deal, so even if they are never drafted, it's a win for them. Only 10% of college players get drafted and play in the minor leagues, and only 750 professional baseball players play in the major leagues each year.

Trading works the same way. There are lessons to be learned, friends to be made in the community of traders, and benefits to be gained from the all research and effort that will make you a better investor, but the simple truth is that most would-be traders are not meant to be. The successful traders I know work 12 hour days, have advanced math skills – I am talking rocket science stuff here, not just being able to figure out the tip quicker that your drinking buddies – massive computing power, and cast iron stomachs with a brutally high pain threshold. If you want a career, wife, kids, outside interests or any other trappings of what we commonly call a "life," you probably are not going to become a successful full time trader.

Trading can be a hobby of sorts, and you may even make a few bucks at it, but odds are you will not make it to the big time. Sorry. That's just how the numbers stack up. Trading is hard. If you have a string of wins, my advice is to cash out and buy some community banks stocks below book value. Keep your trading account relatively small in relation to your net worth. The key to being a long term winner is surviving over the long term.

I will leave you with the single most important lesson I have learned about the stock markets. Cash matters. Holding a high cash balance is how you get filthy, dirty rich. Don't take my word for it. Look at the Forbes list of billionaires. Warren Buffett, Charlie Munger, Andy Beall, Carl Icahn, Leon Black, Sam Zell, Henry Kravis, George Roberts, Robert Bass, Richard Rainwater, Wilbur Ross and countless others have made the list because they had lots of cash on hand and could buy into bear markets. Fortunes are born in market crashes and bloom in bull markets. It is far better to have too much cash in a rising market than too little in a crash. Having cash to buy aggressively when things fall apart is the surest path to getting wealthy in stocks. As Charlie Munger once said, you can look pretty silly sitting around with all that cash – but waiting for exceptional opportunities has been the source of his wealth. Cash matters more than you realize.

DAVE LANDRY

When I first considered learning more about technical analysis and charting back in 2001, a good friend of mine suggested I seek out and learn from Dave Landry. I picked up a few of his books and read some of his daily email recaps, and I was hooked. This guy just spoke to me. He was easy to follow since he wrote in plain English and relied on common sense. I was worried that stepping into a new world with a language all its own would take me years to figure out, but Dave made it easier. Dave's guidance formed the foundation of my knowledge about technical analysis. Dave Landry was the first person who helped me take my game to a new level. To this day, I refer to many of the same time-tested patterns and techniques I learned from studying his notes back when I started. Dave not only wants others to achieve greatness, but he has a passion for teaching, a trait not common among many in the industry. He is often found at seminars and trade shows around the world, divulging his secrets to being successful in trading. Dave Landry can be found at www.davelandry.com, where you can sign up for his powerful email list. You can follow him on Twitter at @davelandrytrdr.

THE POWER OF PERSISTENCE

> *"We shall not cease from exploration, and the end of all our exploring will be to arrive where we started and know the place for the first time"*
>
> *– T.S. Eliot, Four Quartets*

> *"If you advance far enough, you arrive at the beginning."*
>
> – John Bollinger, The Hunt

Nearly all traders tend to go on a Holy Grail hunt, searching for the secret to the markets. They start with a blank chart and began adding indicators. In my case, I began adding indicators to indicators, creating second and even third derivatives – and beyond. The true enlightenment comes when you realize that all you have to do is capture a price move to be successful. Yes, this is easier said than done, but if the ultimate goal is to capture a price movement, then why not focus on price itself? This is why I don't use any indicators other than the occasional moving average.

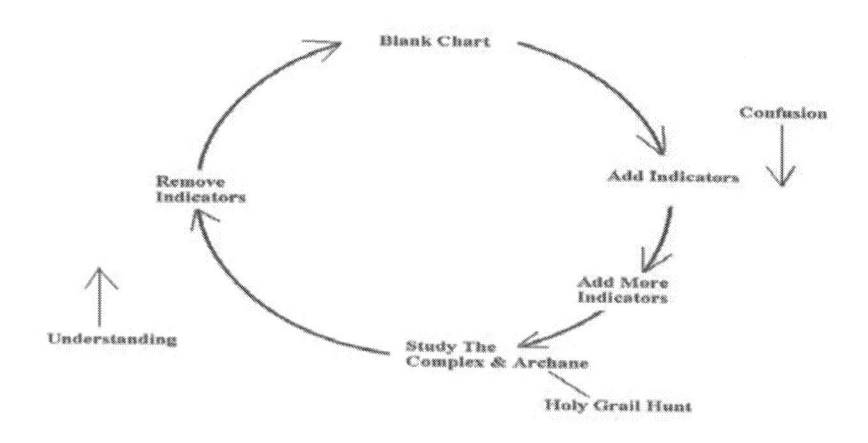

ILLUSTRATE VERSUS INDICATE

Don't get me wrong, there's nothing wrong with indicators. You just need to realize that since they are derived from price they aren't actually "indicating" anything. I like to see them more as "illustrators." They can help to illustrate what's actually happening in price.

PRICE DOESN'T LIE

Once you peel off the indicators, all you're left with is price. Price doesn't lie. It's either going up, down, or sideways. And, since the only way to profit from a trade is to capture a trend, you want to be long when a market is headed higher, short when it's headed lower, and sitting on your hands when it's going sideways. Trading isn't easy, but it's not nearly as difficult as many try to make it. Therefore, if you ever find yourself plotting the third, fourth, or fifth oscillator, come back to price, and only price, and ask yourself: Is the market obviously headed higher? Lower? Or just plain sideways? Never forget that there's nothing magical about a price chart. It simply shows whether the market is in a state of demand (uptrend), supply (downtrend), or equilibrium (sideways).

NEVER FORGET: IT'S EITHER GOING UP, DOWN, OR SIDEWAYS

The back of my business card serves as a constant reminder for me. Whenever I find myself trying to outsmart, outthink, or overcomplicate things I just refer to the card, which I keep tapped to each of my trading monitors.

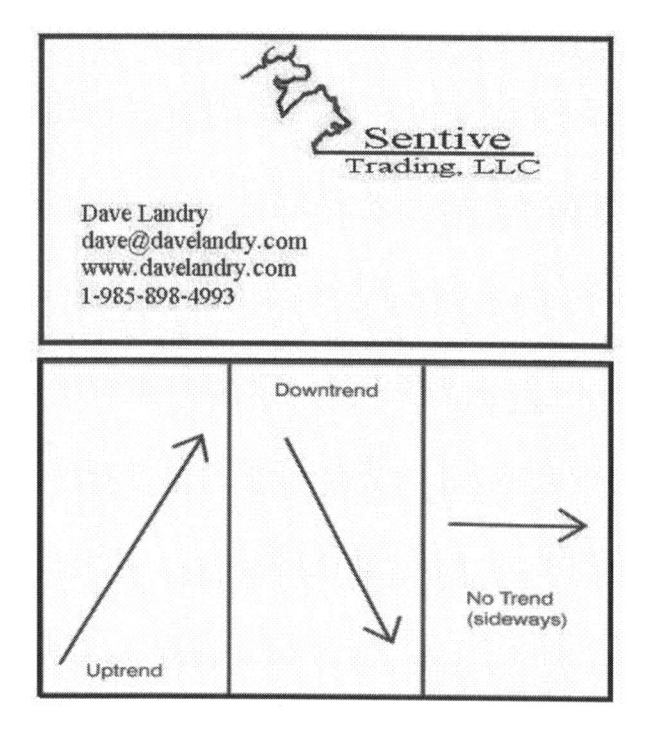

IS PRICE PERSISTING?

One of the simpler concepts that I discovered by focusing mostly on price is the power of persistency. Once you observe that the price is obviously headed in one direction, then ask yourself, "Does the market tend to go up day after day in a fairly straight line?"

A LITTLE BACKGROUND

Before we get into one of my favorite setup combinations using persistency, you'll need a little background to my approach. Referring to Figure 1, nearly all of my setups are pullback related.

I first seek to identify an existing (or emerging*) trend (a) and then look to enter after the market pulls back (b). The reason that I wait for the pullback is that unless you are trading a very large basket of stocks (or other markets), you can't just blindly jump on a trend. Trending markets are prone to corrections. People take profits and eager shorts often pile onboard. And, you never know when these corrections will occur and take you out with them. Therefore, you're much better off waiting for the correction and then looking to enter if, and only if, the trend begins to resume (i.e., an entry).

Waiting for an entry (c) can often keep you out of a losing trade when the correction turns into more than just that (i.e., a top). It also helps to ensure, but obviously not guarantee, that the trend is resuming. Speaking of guarantees or lack thereof, since all trades, no matter how well thought out, have the potential to fail, a protective stop is placed (d) after the entry is triggered. Partial profits are taken (e) just in case the move results in a reversion-to-the-mean type move at best (i.e., a bounce from over- sold). A trailing stop is used (f) and that stop is gradually loosened (g) in an attempt to ride out a longer-term trend on the remainder of the position. Making the transition from the short-term (swing) trader to longer-term trend follower via the trailing stops allows me to "have my cake and eat it too" – to capture both short-term and longer-term moves.

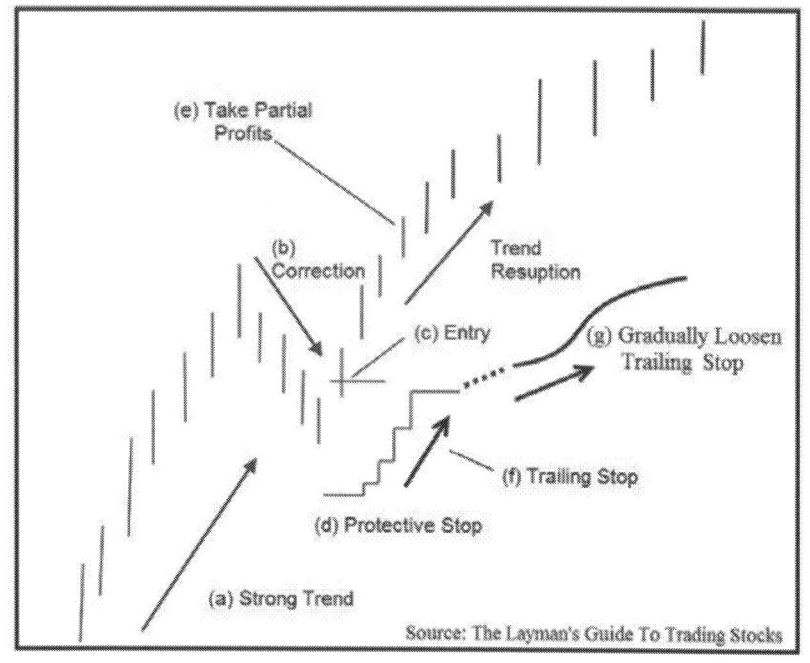

Figure 1

GETTING ONBOARD PERSISTENT TRENDS

Getting back to the concept of persistency: You can measure it mathematically with linear regression. However, again, an indicator just illustrates what's already there. Therefore, I prefer to draw a trend line through the price bars, intersecting as many as possible, as illustrated in Figure 2. Once I identify a persistent trend, I then look to enter on a pullback. For lack of something more eloquent, I have dubbed these "Persistent Pullbacks."

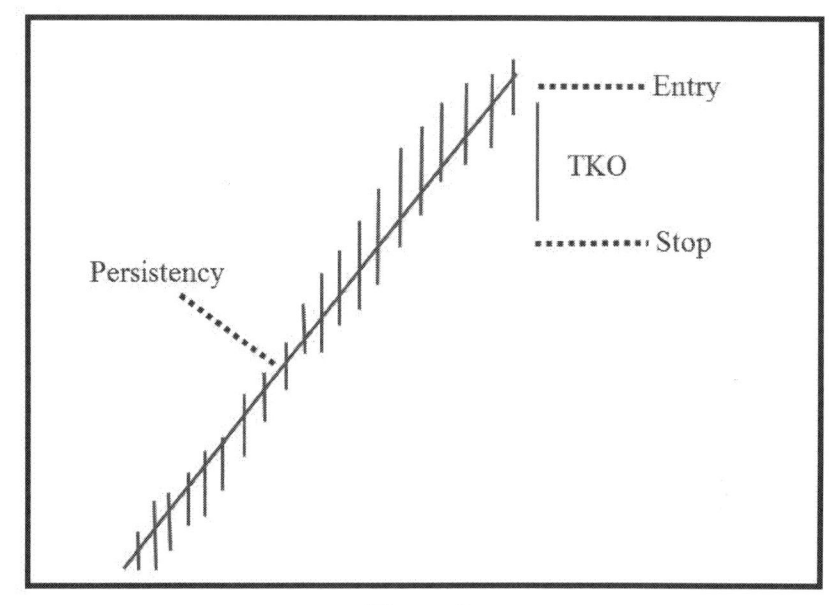

Figure 2

LET'S LOOK AT THE RULES

1. Referring to Figure 2, the market must persist higher for at least 15-20 days (3-4 weeks). A line drawn through the price bars should intersect as many as possible. During this period, the market should have made a considerable move based on its underlying volatility.

2. The market must then pull back. My favorite pullback pattern is a Trend Knockout (TKO). This is where a market in a solid uptrend makes a sharp one-day move lower. This helps to "knock out" the nervous longs (the so called "fast money") and it attracts eager shorts. Should the trend begin to resume, you are able to benefit from the predicament of these traders. The TKO move lower must take out at least the prior two bars and do so in a wide range bar (WRB) fashion. This helps to ensure that some longs have been

knocked out of the market (and shorts have been attracted). This is illustrated in Figure 2. A good litmus test is to ask yourself is this: "If you were long this market, would the TKO move have taken your stop out?"

LET'S LOOK AT AN EXAMPLE

Notice that Celldex Therapeutics (CLDX) is in a persistent trend higher (1). A trend line drawn through the bars intersects most of the bars for over a three-week period. The stock then has a strong one day pullback against the trend (2). This TKO type move has likely both knocked out the weak hands and has attracted some eager shorts. An entry is triggered (3) as the trend begins to resume and a protective stop is placed below the market (4). Short-term profits are taken (5), and the trailing stop on the remainder (6) is gradually loosened in an attempt to ride out a longer-term trend.

Persistent Pullbacks are a very simple yet often quite effective setup. In fact, I would encourage those who are new to trading to trade just this one pattern. It's also a great setup to come back to whenever you find yourself trying to outsmart the market by plotting that third derivative or trying to catch a bottom. By requiring a persistent trend, the setup is self-regulating. You will see little or no buy side setups in bear markets and very few or no setups in sideways choppy markets.

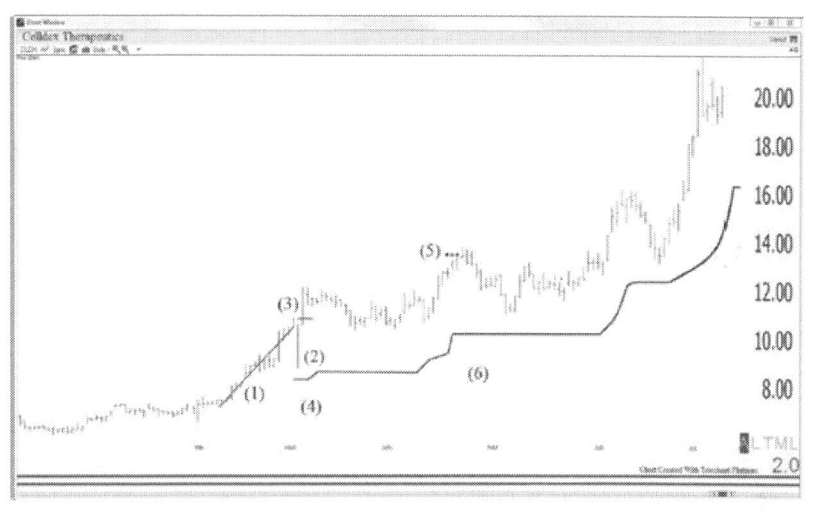

Figure 3

IN SUMMARY

As traders, we all tend to go on the trader's journey, searching for the secret to the markets. This can often lead to making things more complex than they really need to be. The true enlightenment comes when you strip away the indicators and focus on price and only price. Simple priced-based patterns, such as Persistent Pullbacks, can work quite well.

*Note: Emerging (new) trend patterns are slightly more difficult to recognize for the novice. Although the payoff from catching a new trend early can be big, they can be slightly less reliable since the previous trend may still be in place. You are a bit of a "pioneer," seeking to get into a new trend as early as possible. Those newer to trading should focus mostly on existing trend patterns like Persistent Pullbacks.

MISH SCHNEIDER

Mish Schneider is one of the smartest and most experienced women I have come across in my years of trading and investing. She uses a wonderful blend of technicals, charts, good instincts and spot-on timing to find the best ideas for her clients; I find her style both refreshing and enlightening. Mish has years of experience on trading floors, a place where few women are recognized as legitimate. She not only put herself on the line against the male-dominated trading pit but demonstrated a level of skill that kept her customers happy. Today, Mish is an accomplished trader, author and friend to a vast online community. I am proud to share her remarkable story and experiences with you. You can find more from Mish Schneider at www.marketgauge.com, where she blogs daily and provides trade ideas for subscribers. You can follow her on Twitter at @marketminute.

MISH TAKES ON THE WORLD

I got my start in trading "back in the day." Coming out of Queens, New York from a family who scrimped and saved to make the most of a postman's salary, I had zero financial background. I managed to work my way through college and become a special education teacher

Years into my teaching career, I was separated from my first husband, living in a four-story walk-up studio apartment on Manhattan's Upper West Side, and without any money to my name when my life took a twist that changed everything.

I met a neighbor, a young woman who worked on the New York Commodities Exchange as an analyst for Merrill Lynch.

She reported to brokers around the world on who the buyers and sellers of distinction were in Coffee, Sugar and Cocoa.

One day, she brought me down to see the Exchange. My eyes popped out of my head, my heart raced, and the proverbial light bulb shined brightly over my head. I knew right then and there, this is it. I found my calling! Through a somewhat circuitous route, I landed a job working for Paul Sarnoff at Conti-Commodities, Continental Grain's Futures Division.

Mr. Sarnoff placed me on the Coffee, Sugar and Cocoa Exchange doing exactly the same job as my neighbor: Talking on a squawk box to brokers throughout the world about the daily goings on in all three commodity markets. Each afternoon, I wrote commentary, which included both fundamental and technical analysis. That analysis transmitted globally.

Considering I began my auspicious career with zero knowledge and even less money, I made it my business to learn all that I could in the fastest amount of time possible. I became an expert in point and figure charts. I drew x's and o's on graph paper throughout the entire trading session in Sugar Futures. Armed with a piece of cardboard that was 12 inches high by about six inches wide, I then neatly rolled the graph paper onto the cardboard.

From there, I could unravel the roll and identify chart patterns that repeated over and over again. Those chart patterns became my window into how charts not only reflected past price movements, but also how well they could predict probable future price movement. A solid reputation as an expert chartist gave me self-confidence. With money in my pocket for the first time in my life, I opened a trading account.

After my first year on the Floor, Conti-Commodities offered me a seat on the Coffee, Sugar and Cocoa Exchange. I made it to the big time as a broker for a large futures firm. The other members of the Coffee, Sugar and Cocoa Exchange dubbed me "Rookie of the Year!"

A year later Conti got into bed with the Hunt Brothers, who were busily trying to corner the silver market. That did not go too well for them … or for Conti … or for me. I lost my job.

However, my charting skills preceded me and I headed across the floor to Comex to chart for some of the locals and trade for my own account in Silver and Gold Futures. Eventually, I worked my way over to the New York Mercantile Exchange. I leased a seat and remained a local (one who trades for their own account), trading mostly crude oil. By that time, I had nearly six years of experience trading on the floor. In total, I spent twelve years on the floor, eventually leaving to trade "upstairs."

The lessons I learned on the floor remain my foundation for trading today.

On many futures exchanges, unlike equities, the specific commodity opened up month by month. A "pit boss" moderated with the nearest contract month opening first for several minutes. Then, that month would close and each ensuing month opened, following the order of the calendar year. Once the pit boss took the members through each month, the commodity trading would reopen in all months.

This procedure taught me the value of an "opening range." Very often, the price range of the initial open became the range to trade from on the re-open. Over the high of the range brought in more buyers, and under the low of the range brought in more sellers.

The opening range concept has remained a foundation for me and MarketGauge ever since. Regardless of the instrument I am trading, I employ specific rules for how to trade the opening range, implementing a variety of timeframes to wait for: two, five and 30 minutes after the opening bell.

Other invaluable lessons from those days remain my core mantra for success. Determining risk management and risk/reward ratios are paramount for me before executing a position. How volume patterns confirm price movements brings back memories of increasing noise levels in the "pit" when buy or sell stops were hit. The louder the hollers of my pit mates, the better the momentum.

Although I have spent more years sitting at a desk and trading from a computer than I did standing in the pit and yelling out my trades, there remains an unbreakable bond to this day.

Indeed the world and trading are way more complicated now. Yet, in my heart and soul I'm still just one of the "guys" who always made sure they showed up and put their best foot forward. And most importantly, each day we kept our sense of humor as we stood and traded shoulder to shoulder

SKIP RASCHKE

Skip is one of my personal favorites. I love history and hearing stories from the trenches, and Skip has a full bag of them. He started trading options in the early days and cut his teeth on the

floor in Philadelphia. Back then, there was very little liquidity and even less understanding of derivatives as trading tools. To get things rolling, the market needed some trusting and dedicated market makers, and Skip had the vision to see this would be a game where he could win. This vision did not come without risk, and as you'll read below, Skip experienced some frightening moments when it seemed all the risk-taking was for naught. Not many early options traders are still around today, so to say Skip is a survivor is putting it mildly. He is a gifted trader, a warrior, and kind and generous man who is happy to share some of his wisdom. I think you'll find Skip's stories fascinating. He is a colleague of mine at realmoney.com. To read more from Skip, go to his blog at www.sotdaily.com.

AN EPIPHANY LIKE NO OTHER!

Epiphany: a usually sudden manifestation or perception of the essential nature or meaning of something.

My *epiphany* occurred when I was "working" in an options trading pit on the floor of the Philadelphia Stock Exchange in early 1983. I was then a newly designated professional options trader, making markets on designated stocks' options. Basically, I had bankrolled myself to trade options for my own risk and reward – and life! The place I chose was Philadelphia (the PHLX), which was about 2,800 miles from home. All of my friends and, of course, relatives declared that I had gone nuts. I deferred arguing their point.

A professional trader is like no other type of trader in that if they succeed, all is well, if not greatly so. But if they fail, they don't eat well and might eventually get wiped out. Maybe "do or die" fits the range of potentials? Ah yes, it does.

Fear of being wiped out, financially speaking, is a great motivator (hell, fear of not eating well is enough to motivate me!). Once that fear hits you, your brain begins to think like never before. Personal survival has a way of doing that since well before Darwin wrote about the importance of being one of the fittest – or else. Every spare moment becomes a time to think and try to find the edge (any edge!) in a trade that might be setting up. Or to maybe discover an untested tactic with real money (yours!), employing that new tactical approach as you risk real money (yours!) that can go "poof" in the process of taking that risky, newly formed path to options trading nirvana.

Any real pro, one who makes the "cut," so to speak, knows that the reward potential for any trade being considered takes a back seat to first determining if the risk is worth it. For a pro, the path taken is risk assessed first, while reward is relegated to being a possible bonus at best.

The "retail" trader's mentality tends to be in reverse, as the retail mind's critical path of thinking about a trade has reward well ahead of risk. That is just one way that retail-minded traders fail over time. And it is why the pro has the staying power required for ultimate success in trading.

So, what was my epiphany during that one trading day in early 1983? A bit of background is necessary in order to do justice to the story: That day, I would short 5,000 shares of Waste Management (I scaled into that total during the day). Back then, that short sale had to be executed on upticks in the stock (the Uptick Rule was stupidly eliminated by the SEC in 2007). Upticks can be fickle, especially in an actively traded growth stock (Waste Management, or WM, was a nifty fifty stock back then, akin today to maybe Facebook's trading action).

That morning, WM was overbought and had some downside work to do. The WM option volatilities were trading near their lows.

Now, a market maker must buy on their bid and sell on their offer. But, they don't have to be masochistic about it! Our floor rules required each market maker to trade "10 lots" on all bids and offers if a market order hit the bid or wanted to take the offer. Thus, many times I (and the other four traders in my pit) had to "stand up" to our posted bids and offers to the tune of 10 contracts (thus five traders buy/sell two contracts each).

WM was readying to test lower levels, which was not missed by those who traded the stock from off the floor (experienced firm traders, hedge fund traders, etc.). Thus, some of them would sell at the money calls and then maybe use the credit from premium gathered when calls were sold short (we were buying them) to buy put protection. Over time, and on this day in particular, plenty of off-floor call selling was coming into our pit, and thus, we were those calls' buyers. By 2pm that day, I had bought 100 at the money calls, which, if not hedged, had me long 5,000 WM deltas in a stock most likely preparing to go lower. Ugh was the word. It seemed that every trader who knew the stock was doing one of two things: going short or hedging for the downside yet to come. And of course WM was not upticking much either.

I had a standing order with my NYSE broker in the WM pit to short 5,000 shares of WM "not held." A not held order given to a broker is sort of like giving a grenade without a pin to a kid with the shakes. Nothing against brokers, but they are, ah, brokers and not traders. (That's why any time you hear a floor broker on CNBC shoot their mouth off about the market, a stock, hell a horse if we're talking about the fifth race at Del Mar, you mute him!)

Back to the story. Since the calls were smashed as the vols (volatility) were trashed, I wound up buying 100 at the money calls for a very low volatility. Thus, that risk mostly already absorbed by buying the calls at what I still label as "wholesale" price levels. But I was still long 5,000 deltas!

Then, somehow as if by divine providence, I receive an execution ticket from my NYSE broker in the WM pit that I had shorted those 5,000 shares at a very decent price of $55 (relative to the previously accumulated buy cost of the calls). Yeah! I was hedged off, and at a delta-neutral number level (zero is delta neutral). And I had tons of positive gamma (the position of long 100 at the money calls and short the stock is loaded with positive gamma in both price directions and theta).

Seven days later, WM hadn't moved much, and I had not screwed around with that position (the position being what is called, by me, a "dynamic synthetic put"). Thus, that theta was in play but not yet burning money. However, the clock was ticking on the life of those long at the money calls. It felt like tepid water slowly approaching the boiling stage.

Now, each morning a pro options trader gets his or her "sheets," which show all of the previous day's activity (trades), from a clearing firm. You also get all of the positions in numerical and graphed form (the "what if" graphs). At the bottom of the numerical run is a section called "short stock credit balance." Because I had never shorted a stock as a pro, I had never before seen any money in that "short stock credit balance" section. That morning my sheet read $316. Huh. What was that? A mistake no doubt. Thus, off I went to find the answer as to who the real recipient of that $316 was, as it couldn't be me.

My clearing firm's head of operations sat me down and began to explain how I had accumulated that $316. OMG! What? That was MY money?

She said that all stocks sold create a credit (duh # 1 for me), and that all credit balances must be paid interest (duh # 2 for me). Short sales of stock create credit balances just like long sales of stock create credit balances. Every time I short stock, like the previous day's short sale of 5,000 shares at 55 in WM, I will be paid interest on that credit balance total. *Hallelujah*! I had found the Lost City of Cibola! It was located at 20th and Market Street in Philadelphia!

Ok, so here was that math as best I can recall (I do have an eidetic memory, but this was almost 33 years ago): Selling short 5,000 shares at 55 creates a credit balance of $275,000. The rate of interest back then was 6% (APR). Divide 6% by 365 days. Take that result times $275,000 (the credit balance) times 7 (the days I was being paid the daily interest) equaled the $316 credit. (Got all that math? Yeah, it took me a few minutes too!)

OMG, I thought. Now, how many more times can I do this and how much money will my clearing firm allow me to risk by doing so? In other words, how much leverage will my clearing firm give me for each dollar of my own that I have n the account?

That answer – how much could I short til my head caves in – would determine my new religion, err, strategy!

Over time my clearing firm accepted a peak leverage ratio of 20-1 for my account. Thus, for each dollar I had in the account (mine), the clearing firm would lend me $19. But they would only do so if their total risk was actually my total risk relative to the cash I kept in the account. In simple terms, I could blow every dollar in the account and my clearing firm would not lose a dime in the process. But that was where the buck (risked by the clearing firm) literally stopped. I thought this was fair, and someday when I grow up, I want to be a clearing firm!

Over time (like 10 years of it), my average annual profit (net) from my short stock credit balances averaged over $100,000 annually. Thus, that epiphany, that first day when this all came together in my head (and wallet) was quite the day that I will always remember – with one huge smile on my face!

Chapter 15 Takeaways

- *Steve Burns teaches you the importance of mastering trading discipline.*

- *Tim Melvin shares with you the value investor approach, which relies on being patient and letting companies (like community banks) do their thing.*

- *Dave Landry walks you through his favorite technical strategies, including following price action and using the Persistent Pullback to spot winners*

- *Mish Schneider became a commodities trader by happy accident, but she became an expert technician on purpose – expertise that has earned her a successful career as a trader.*

- *Skip Raschke learned early on the beauty of short stock credit balances – and he's still hoping to be a clearing firm one day.*

CHAPTER 16

Ready to Trade? You Need to Fill Your Toolbox

You've learned pretty much everything you need to know about options trading. Now it's time to learn how to execute trades.

START WITH A COMFORTABLE CUSHION OF SAVINGS

First things first: you need to fund a trading account with an optimal amount of capital. If you wish to be a full-time trader and make a living at the game, there is much to consider.

I suggest that any trader, regardless of skill level, have at least one year's worth of expenses saved; two years is better. Say your monthly expenses total $4,000. You need to keep at least $50,000 separate from your trading account, though $75,000 is more comfortable.

Why be so conservative? You will no doubt find yourself in challenging situations with tough decisions to make. You will face events that are out of your control. You could suffer sharp losses. Think about the Great Recession of 2009. Many traders were caught off guard and paid dearly. Those who were prepared lived to fight another day.

TIE YOUR TRADING CAPITAL TO YOUR EXPECTED EARNINGS

The amount of capital you trade with depends on the type of products you are trading. Because of the leverage opportunities you have with futures and options, they require less capital (and risk) than stocks. Equities have an even better risk management profile than options.

You also need to take into consideration how much you want to earn. Let's say your goal is to make $100,000 in one year. That may seem like a pie-in-the-sky goal, but it really depends on how much capital you are starting with. If you have $50,000 to trade with, doubling your money will be very hard. You'll have to be right nearly every day. If you have $200,000 to trade with, you have much more room to breathe – and much less pressure to be "perfect" (which we know is impossible) every day.

Back to the annual goal of $100,000. That may seem like a big number, so just break it down. On a monthly basis, you would have to earn $8,300 or so, and on a weekly basis, you would have to earn $2,100. Drill down to daily, and you're looking at $420. Much easier to digest, right? You can make $420 with just one trade every day – but let's not forget that losses can and will happen.

BE DISCIPLINED

Earning that $420 each day requires skill, focus, and discipline. Can you be happy "just" making $420, or will you continue to go to the well for more action? A disciplined trader knows when it is time to stop trading, and a well-capitalized trader will find it much easier to deal with the losses. You need to be both disciplined and well-capitalized. Unfortunately, I've seen far too many under-capitalized traders completely lose control – and it ain't pretty.

CHOOSE A TRADING PLATFORM

Brokers like TD Ameritrade, E-Trade, Fidelity and Interactive Brokers offer some of the best tools for all levels of traders. The platform you choose is entirely up to you, but here are the features to look for

- An easy-to-use platform with a full suite of tools
- An online platform that adapts to mobile devices so you can trade from anywhere (that has a good WiFi connection)
- Competitive commission rates
- Services such as charting and educational webinars and other content
- Compatibility with your computer's operating system

INVEST IN SOME MONITORS

I have seen traders use as many as 30 monitors – I kid you not! That seems like overkill, but some traders need to keep tabs on multiple charts and trading platforms. For most traders three to six monitors is ideal, but again, that depends on what you are trading. Start with three. If you need more, you can buy more.

LINE UP EDUCATIONAL RESOURCES

To get an edge, you need to find the best sources of education and information. I have listed some of my favorite resources in the next chapter, but of course it isn't an exhaustive list. There are so many websites, blogs, webinars, and podcasts out there. Find the ones that make sense and work for you – and commit to learning every single day.

CHAPTER 17

My Reading List

One of the hardest parts of being a trader is constantly managing the flow of market information. It certainly helps to keep an ear to the ground at all times. You might hear something relevant to your current position or a new trading idea that is worth investigating. Of course, you cannot possibly know everything that is going on, but you can manage where and from whom you receive information to maximize that information flow. It's all about relevancy, accuracy and timeliness.

Below you'll find a list of the websites I follow daily, weekly, or monthly. Some you need to pay for, some are a hybrid of free and paid. Those that require a paid subscription are marked with $$$, and those that offer a hybrid are marked with $. As always, some information is not pertinent to you, so use your best judgment.

DAILY

stockwinners.com: Relevant and timely breaking news about companies, individuals and trading ideas, both stocks and options. $$$

trade-alert.com: Option order flow of various sizes that I use to assess where the big money is flowing. $$$

hardrightedge.com: Solid market commentary by author and swing trader Alan Farley and a collection of several very good technicians. I use this site to learn about different trading patterns.

realmoney.com: The paid subscription site for thestreet.com offers a strong lineup of investing and trading pros who supply their own take on the markets. Jim Cramer and Doug Kass frequently contribute. $$$

stockcharts.com: An incredibly easy and valuable charting tool founded by famed technician John Murphy; this is where I do most of my charting work. $$$

thestreet.com: An enormous collection of articles that range from fundamental to technical to relevant data and output. An ideal portal for market junkies.

bloomberg.com: Relevant and timely news articles about world markets and breaking news events.

investing.com: A nice collection of global bloggers with different perspectives and a great source of timely economic data releases and assessments.

briefing.com: Up-to-date earnings releases and estimates. It's also a good site for economic data analysis. $

Investors.com The digital format of Investors Business Daily includes a wealth of learning tools for the novice up to the expert. One of the best layouts you will find.

Twitter: Rapid fire information is disseminated daily over this social network. By following some of the best and most reliable investors and traders, I have several sets of eyes finding and sharing information that help me make better decisions.

Facebook: Some very good traders and investors share information on this site as well

tradingvolatility.net: The best place to follow the volatility term structure for VIX Russell 2000, Nasdaq and Stoxx (Euro). Jay Wolberg has the best display of information and the most powerful tools in this area. Some free, but the paid version is worth it. $

WEEKLY

marketmonograph.com: A weekly data compilation by Fred Goodman that expands into a slew of technical indicators, economic analysis and several charts, giving you a very good view of where markets are heading. I have found it to be some of the best and most precise data. $$$

mauldin economics: John Mauldin has been writing about markets for years. He distills his thoughts into a free weekly newsletter, but the true value is in the knowledge shared on his website. He has also authored several books; my favorite is *Endgame*

fibonacciqueen.com: Carolyn Boroden is truly the queen of fibonacci and time series analyses. Her approach is based on criterion that is simple to understand, and her analysis is spot on. She is also an amazing teacher. $$$

MONTHLY OR PERIODICALLY

riskreversal.com: Run by CNBC Fast Money contributor Dan Nathan, you'll find some great trading ideas, superior learning tools, and excellent information about options. $$$

optionpit.com: Mark Sebastian is an expert at analyzing volatility. This is a great learning site if you want to expand your knowledge about the VIX and volatility structures. $

artoftrading.net: The focus here is on the psychology of trading from a veteran trader. Trader Stewie (@traderstewie on Twitter) is always kind, helpful, and straightforward. $

cboe.com: A wealth of educational material including blogs, seminars, webinars and news updates. Some of the best writers are found at CBOE.

optionsprofits.com: The paid options section of realmoney.com is managed by Jill Malandrino. She collects information from some of the best-known options players around, and the site is filled with videos, articles, blogs, and a chat forum for users.

cnbc.com: A great site for up to date information about markets. All of the information is compiled around segments and guests, and the video clips and articles are timely.

traderplanet.com: A tremendous collection of some of the best minds on Wall Street with great articles on relevant topics.

ivolatility.com: The best site for historical and implied volatility data, including up to date activity and readings.

wsj.com: All the market action in one spot, including news events and breaking ideas from some of the best market writers. Follow @wsj on Twitter for trading ideas.

Chapter 17 Takeaway

- *Read all you can to become better at trading and investing – but be careful to not become overwhelmed by too much information.*

CHAPTER 18

Case Studies

I have been crafting my technical analysis skills for years, and I measure my progress with actual results, not hypothetical stories. Below are some bullish case studies that allowed the Explosive Options community of traders to post big wins. I've also included a bear case study to demonstrate that yes, you can win during a bear market.

GOPRO – 2014

GoPro went public in early summer 2014 and was celebrated as the next great hardware company. When stock finally became available for ownership, investors were determined to get a piece of the pie.

The stock chart below shows where this stock was ready to move.

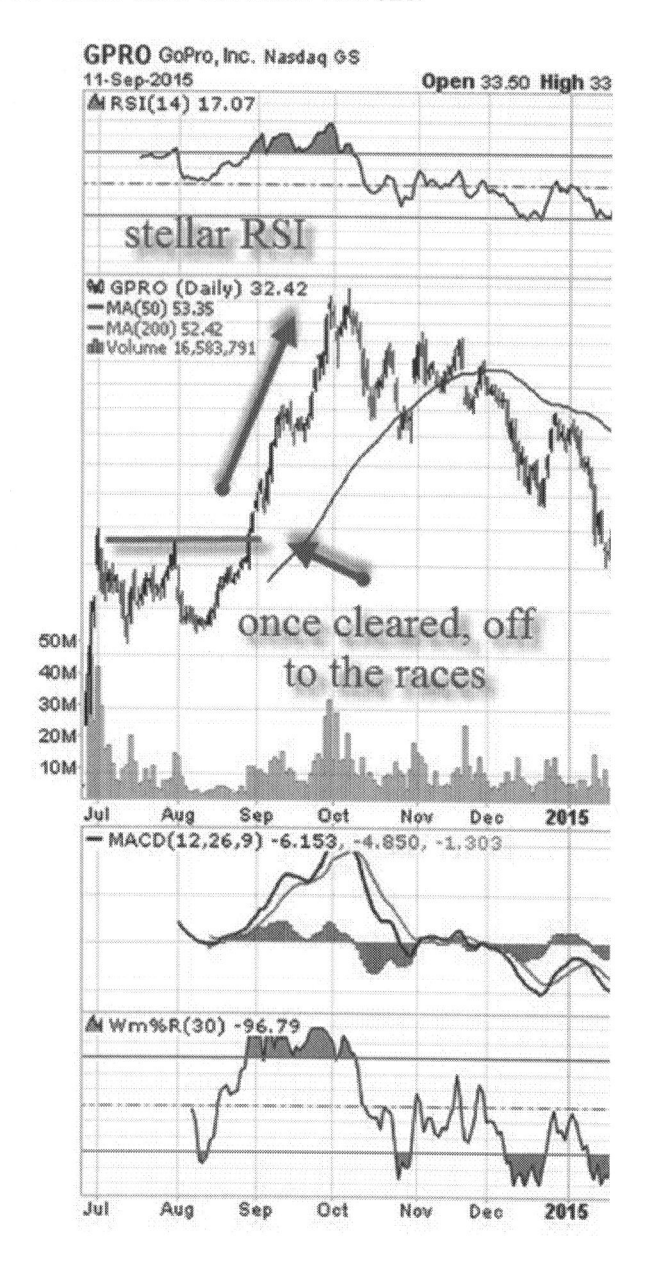

After a slight rest period in late summer, I started to take notice of the charts, technicals and specific indicators. Initially, some levels needed to be exceeded before a good run could ensue. A small window of opportunity appeared as the stock moved around the low 40's range. A tight price area was here, but a breakout would be imminent when price closed near 50. We put on a call trade in mid-August.

Four days later, we sold the trade for a nice gain. Why did we exit this trade when we did? The name of the game is to book profits when we have them, and an 80% win in a few short days was enough for us, thank you very much! In addition, we could "reset" and look for another trade, which is exactly what we did.

The stock was really starting to get moving, and with such good performance from the indicators, it was time to get in again just days later. We held onto this new trade and in just 10 days booked an amazing 225% winner on an October option.

We still saw more upside to come, so we went out even further to January, which would capture a potentially strong holiday shopping season. Our January 50 call purchase was on fire from the start, and we never looked back until we sold it.

After booking this 151% gain, we were easily playing each subsequent position with **house money**. The last trade was a 160% winner, and we were done. The chart looked rather **toppy** and since we had dipped into the well four times, we didn't want to push our luck. All told, we booked four winners for a total of more than 600% in gains.

Clearly this was a smashing winner, and we saw the potential in the charts. Even though the fundamentals preached that the stock was well over-valued, GoPro made us money – and that's all that mattered.

More details on these trades are in the blog entry at: http://explosiveoptions.net/2014/08/lights-camera-action-gopro-ready-big-move-higher/

ALIBABA – 2014

The biggest IPO in history belongs to Alibaba Group, the Chinese online retailer that boasts well over 300 million users. Before going public in September 2014, the company was the envy of retailers everywhere, with operating margins well over 40%, slim inventory and burgeoning growth prospects. The anticipation of its IPO was fascinating to observe, and like GoPro, investors could not wait to get on board.

We saw a huge opportunity to buy into this name in October after the market severely corrected. (The SPX 500 fell more than 9% mostly due to uncertainty over the Ebola Virus.) The Alibaba chart showed some good support in the mid 80's range, even though the stock had been falling daily following the successful IPO.

Like GoPro, this was ready to launch once it exceeded some resistance levels, in this case around the 90 area. The technicals were favorable, and since the issue was rather new, there was little in the way of resistance. Volume was also starting to swell (it's always a good sign when volume levels are high – it means the stock is breaking out on price).

With market momentum acting as wind in its sails, we entered the trade cautiously, adding a Dec 90 call in October at 5.70, and selling about ten days later for an 80% win (out at 10.45). This trade was about risk management and not being greedy. At this point, we saw more upside to come, but we wanted more time to let the trade work.

We came back with a Jan 100 call buy at 6, and once again the stock went on a relentless run higher. A week later, we booked another huge winner. We decided to cool it off from here, as the stock had been running hard and was due for a rest.

A YouTube video was created for this trade example, you can view it at the link below

https://www.youtube.com/watch?v=zJIvYxKjknM

In addition, a complete review of the trade analysis can be seen at the link below

http://explosiveoptions.net/alibaba-case-study/

GOOGLE – 2015

Our Google call plays in summer 2015 were some of the best ever at Explosive Options. The mind-boggling gains in such a short period of time were talked about for months in the chat room after the trade was over!

On July 16, Google's Q2 earnings were released after the close, and though revenue was a bit light, bottom line earnings were solid. The stock moved to new highs the following day, Google enjoyed its biggest gain in 2 ½ years, and it vaulted up to the second biggest market cap company behind Apple.

While we (me and members of the chat room) recognized the strong fundamentals, we saw something very positive in the charts/technicals prior to the earnings release that made the decision to get on board a bit easier.

On July 10, I had my first clue that something may be happening. The stock had been building up some compression for months, moving in a narrow channel within a wider one. Even when the stock's move up toward $560 was rejected, it did not break down.

With these conditions, getting in on a Google trade was not easy. We already had a position on July monthly 570 calls and were looking another play. However, we were comfortable adding an out of the money play to the Explosive Options portfolio; specifically, the July 24 (weekly) option long at $7.

By the following Tuesday, July 14, Google had vaulted higher on strong turnover, and with earnings due out later in the week, it appeared many traders were positioning for a substantial move up. Our new calls were now up nearly 200% in just three days, so as we always like to do, we took our risk off the table to stay in the game. We sold this call for a very nice gain and rolled up to a higher strike, removing our risk entirely. If the trade were to flop, we still would end up a winner. We ended up buying the July 24 weekly 600 strike call at 5.10.

At this point, we were long a call going into earnings. That may bother some traders (due to the expected price action/ volatility that we see after a report), but since we had a "free trade" on the table, we were in a good position – no matter what the result. The strategy worked. On Friday, July 17, the stock soared over 16%, and our calls went up an astounding 15x! Just buying ONE contract at 5.10 for 510 bucks would have netted you over $8,100 in profits or an astonishing 1,600% return!

But that's not the full story. Prior to earnings I noticed a very familiar and distinct fat tail pattern. Google was set up perfectly for upside on this basis alone. Take a look at the charts prior to earnings and then after earnings, and you'll see that fat tail. Knowing this pattern was a great guidepost.

You can find the full story in this blog post:

http://explosiveoptions.net/options-trading-strategies/win-big-google/

INDEX PUTS – 2015

As you know from earlier chapters, I am a huge advocate of always having some protection. This story illustrates why you are very glad to have it when market volatility starts to rise.

Coming into late summer 2015, the markets seemed on edge. For most of the year, the SPX 500 had been trading in a wide range, hitting 2040 to the downside and 2135 to the upside. Each challenge to the lower end was scooped up by buyers, causing stocks to head upward. However, in late August that lower bound did not hold. News surfaced that China was devaluing its currency and had suspect growth projections, and that was enough to break the dam.

We had some insurance via index puts, mostly SPY (the SPX 500 proxy), DIA (Dow Industrials 30 proxy) and IWM (Russell 2000). While the market volatility was starting to rise, these puts also started to gain in value. We took a gain in late August and rolled these down to lower strike prices on Friday, August 21, not knowing what would unfold during the next session.

On Monday, August 24, the markets went haywire. Futures markets were selling off relentlessly just prior to the market open (futures markets trade overnight and are used as a market proxy). A massive **market crash** ensued at the open. The Dow Industrials tumbled more than 1,000 points but quickly recovering many of those losses.

The puts we had bought on Friday (rolled down) paid off with huge gains, and we used the selloff to take them off the table. That morning the VIX climbed to 53, a level not seen since 2008.

Now, clearly we didn't expect this drop to occur with such severity, but being protected with puts certainly was helpful as the event played out.

CHAPTER 19

The Mad Money Experience

> *"As long as you enjoy investing, you'll be willing to do the homework and stay in the game. That's why I try to make the show so entertaining, because if you aren't interested, you'll either miss the opportunity to make money in the market or not pay enough attention and end up losing your shirt."*
>
> *– Jim Cramer*

In March 2015, I had the pleasure of joining Jim Cramer and his crew to celebrate the 10th anniversary of Mad Money on CNBC. It was an amazing event, with a live in-studio audience and a special call-in by Apple CEO Tim Cook. The show has enjoyed an incredible run through a boom cycle, the Great Recession, a recovery to all-time highs, and important issues in between.

No matter what the markets are doing, Jim Cramer has done everything to keep everyone in the game, but he directs most of his attention to the average working-class American. He wants to help everyone be smarter, and he repeats his mantra for the "home gamers" often: Do your homework (his saying is 'buy and homework' rather than 'buy and hold'). He understands that this demographic is the bread and butter of the country. To bring investing to this group, dubbed **Cramericans**, day after day and present concepts in a way that is easy to understand explains why the show has been on the air for so long.

Take the weekly "Off the Charts" segment, when Jim offers a brief dive into the world of technical analysis. For many, charting and technicals are a mystery. Big money managers pay attention to charts, so why shouldn't everyone learn about them? Since October 2012, Jim and his crew have called on me to provide some valuable knowledge and ideas to his viewers. We've had success highlighting Boeing, Goldman Sachs, casinos, **FANG** (Facebook, Amazon, Netflix and Google), and even the energy sector, Euro and retail/restaurant stocks. The segment is one of the most popular of the week (Tim Collins, Carley Garner, Carolyn Boroden and Ed Ponsi, to name a few, also appear on Off the Charts).

In August 2014, I was asked to appear live with Jim on the show for "Chart Week." To this day, this show is the ONLY time outsiders other than company executives have appeared on Mad Money. During my appearance, we profiled the above-mentioned FANG stocks, which had risen sharply since we first profiled them in 2013. The segment was educational and fun, kicking off an exciting week of technical analysis.

I am truly honored to be called upon regularly for Off the Charts. Like Jim Cramer I am all about teaching and educating so others can reach their financial goals.

Chapter 19 Takeaways

- *Jim Cramer is the eminent go-to guy for investment education, and Mad Money is a great resource for learning the basics of investing.*

- *Jim believes everyone can create wealth from the stock market in a very methodical, disciplined and strategic fashion.*

Glossary

Accumulation/distribution: A tool that measures the trend in buying (accumulation) or selling (distribution) pressure in a security. When the line is trending up, it's a signal of increasing buying pressure, as the stock is closing above the halfway point of the range. If the line is trending downward, it's a signal of increasing selling pressure.

All in: A term typically used in poker, it refers to putting all of one's chips into the pot and risking your remainder on one hand. For traders, it means a heavy investment in one position.

Analysis paralysis: Caused by over-analyzing (or overthinking) a situation to the point that a decision cannot be made. In effect, it paralyzes the outcome.

At the money: An option's strike price is identical to the price of the underlying security. Both call and put options are simultaneously "at the money."

Back 'n fill: This occurs after the market hits a low, holds the low, and trades sideways.

Bollinger bands: Developed by famous technical trader John Bollinger, this measurement plots two standard deviations away from a moving average.

Bollinger bandwidth: Measures the percentage difference between the upper band and the lower band. Bandwidth decreases as bollinger bands narrow and increases as bollinger bands widen. Because bollinger bands are based on the standard deviation, falling bandwidth reflects decreasing volatility and rising bandwidth reflects increasing volatility.

Calendar spread: A trade that involves simultaneously buying a put and a call of the same underlying stock and strike price but with different expiration dates.

Call: Call options allow you to buy at certain price. As the buyer, you want the stock to go up. As the seller, you want the stock to go down.

Collar: A protective options strategy that is implemented after a long position in a stock has experienced substantial gains. It is created by buying an out of the money put option while simultaneously selling an out of the money call option

Correlation: In the world of finance, a statistical measure of how two securities move n relation to each other

Covered call option: A transaction in which the seller of call options owns the corresponding amount of the underlying instrument, such as shares of a stock or other securities

Cup and handle: A chart pattern that resembles a cup with a handle. The cup is in the shape of a "U" and the handle has a slight downward drift, indicating low trading volume. These patterns can last as short as seven weeks and as long as 65 weeks. When you see this pattern occur, it means a stock has moved up to test old highs. When it does, the stock will incur selling pressure by the people who bought at or near the old high. This selling pressure will make the stock price trade sideways with a tendency towards a downtrend before it takes off and moves higher.

Death cross: Occurs when a long-term moving average crosses a short-term moving average in a negative direction (to the downside). It is interpreted as a decisive downturn in the market

Diagonal calendar spread: A trade that involves simultaneously buying a put and a call of the same underlying stock that have different strike prices and different expiration dates. When you buy the longer-dated option, you buy the diagonal spread.

Double bottom: The pattern is formed by two price minima separated by a local peak defining the neck line. The formation is completed and confirmed when the price rises above the neck line, indicating that further price rise is imminent or highly likely.

Double top: Two consecutive peaks of approximately the same price on a price-versus-time chart. The two peaks are separated by a minimum in price, also referred to as a valley or the neckline of the double top formation. The formation is completed and confirmed when the price falls below the neck line, indicating that further price decline is imminent or highly likely.

Dry powder: A slang term that refers to marketable securities that are highly liquid and considered cash-like, such as Treasury notes. Dry powder may also refer to cash reserves kept on hand to cover future obligations or purchase assets.

Elliott wave theory: Ralph Nelson Elliott developed this theory in the late 1920s. He discovered that stock markets traded in repetitive cycles (rather than pure chaos) caused by investors' reactions to outside influences, or predominant psychology of the masses. Putting two and two together, he posited that upward and downward swings of mass psychology always showed up in the same repetitive patterns, which were subdivided into patterns he termed "waves."

Exchange-Traded Fund (ETF): A marketable security that tracks an index, a commodity, bonds, or a basket of assets like an index fund. Unlike mutual funds, an ETF trades like a common stock on a stock exchange. ETFs experience price changes throughout the day as they are bought and sold.

FANG: An acronym that stands for Facebook, Amazon, Netflix and Google.

Fat tails: An extreme probability distribution. For trading purposes, it refers to a stock that moves swiftly up in in value.

Frequency distribution: A table that displays the frequency of various outcomes in a sample. Each entry in the table includes how frequently a value occurs within a particular group or interval. As a result, the table summarizes the distribution of values in the sample.

Golden cross: Occurs when a short-term moving average crosses a major long-term moving average in a positive direction (to the upside). It is interpreted as a definitive upward turn in the market.

Great Recession: A period of global economic decline observed that began following the 2007-08 global financial crisis. The exact scale and timing of the **recession** is debated and varies from country to country.

Greeks: A group of terms that use Greek letters to represent the sensitivity of derivative prices, including options, to risk (or a change in underlying parameters on which the value of an instrument or portfolio of financial instruments is dependent).

Historical volatility: A measure of the volatility of the underlying stock. It is "known" volatility, because it is based on actual, recent price changes.

House money: A common gambling term. In trading, it means you're putting your original investment back into your pocket (so you have no risk of losing it) and are keeping the proceeds from your investment in a security. Even if you lose it all, you still have your original investment

Implied volatility: A function of an option's price. It shows the expectation of future volatility.

Index put options: An option contract in which the holder (buyer) has the right (but not the obligation) to sell a specified quantity of a security at a specified price (strike price) within a fixed period of time (until its expiration).

Initial Public Offering (IPO): The first sale of stock by a company to the public. IPOs are often issued by smaller, younger companies seeking capital to expand. As part of an IPO, the issuer obtains the assistance of an underwriting firm, which helps it determine what type of security to issue (common or preferred), the best offering price, and the time to bring it to market

Intrinsic value: The portion of an option that has real value as opposed to time value.

Leverage: For trading purposes, it means borrowing capital to make an investment and expecting that the profits earned will be greater than the interest paid.

Liquidity: For trading purposes, a high volume of trading activity.

Macro: Large-scale issues

Market crash: A sudden and dramatic decline of stock prices across a significant cross-section of the stock market, resulting in a significant loss of paper wealth. Crashes are driven by panic as much as by underlying economic factors. They often follow speculative stock market bubbles.

Market maker: A broker-dealer firm that accepts the risk of holding a certain number of shares of a particular security in order to facilitate trading in that security. Each market maker competes for customer order flow by displaying buy and sell quotations for a guaranteed number of shares.

Market multiple: Analysis performed to determine if a stock is appropriately priced. It's usually calculated by dividing the stock price by the earnings per share for a particular period.

Naked call option: An option contract that does not include ownership of the underlying security by the buyer or seller. (It is the opposite of a covered option.)

Open interest: The total number of options and/or futures contracts that are not closed or delivered on a particular day.

Option contract: An agreement between a buyer and seller that gives the option buyer the right to buy or sell a particular asset at a later date at an agreed upon price. Option contracts are often used in securities, commodities, and real estate transactions.

Option premium: The amount an option buyer pays to buy a call or put based in the amount of intrinsic and/or time premium offered by the option seller.

Options expiration: The date when index and equity options expire. The actual expiration is always a Saturday, but all trading must be concluded by the market close on Friday.

Options: A financial derivative that represents a contract sold by one party (option writer) to another party (option holder). The contract offers the buyer the right, but not the obligation, to buy (call) or sell (put) a security or other financial asset at an agreed-upon price (the strike price) during a certain period of time or on a specific date (exercise date).

Opportunity cost: The loss of potential gain when one alternative is chosen.

Out of the money A call option with a strike price that is higher than the market price of the underlying asset, or a put option with a strike price that is lower than the market price of the underlying asset. An out of the money option has no intrinsic value, but only possesses extrinsic or time value. As a result, the value of an out of the money option erodes quickly with time as it gets closer to expiration. If it's still out of the money at expiration, the option will expire worthless.

Put: Put options allow you to sell at a certain price. As the buyer, you want the stock to go down. As the seller, you want the stock to go up.

Risk: Expose something of value, like your portfolio, to loss.

Stock market: The market in which shares of publicly held companies are issued and traded either through exchanges or over-the-counter markets. Also known as the equity market, the stock market is one of the most vital components of a free-market economy, as it provides companies with access to capital in exchange for a slice of ownership in the company.

Straddle: A neutral strategy in options trading that involve simultaneously buying a put and a call of the same underlying stock, strike price and expiration date.

Strangle: The purchase or sale of options that allow the holder to profit based on how much the price of the underlying security moves, with relatively minimal exposure to the direction of price movement.

Technical analysis: Methodology used to forecast the direction of prices through the study of past market data, primarily price and volume.

Time value: The portion of an option's value derived from a mathematical equation (such as the Black Scholes Model) that is based on the amount of time remaining in the life of an option. Since time value of an option is outside intrinsic value there is no 'true value' of the option that could be exercised, as the option is out of the money. Only in the money options can be exercised

Toppy: A slang term used to describe markets that are reaching unstable highs, and therefore a decline can be expected. In the US, those markets include the Dow Jones Industrial Average, the Nasdaq, and the S&P 500.

Valuation: The current worth of an asset or company

VIX: The Volatility Index (VIX) is a contrarian sentiment indicator that helps to determine when too much optimism or fear is in the market. When sentiment reaches one extreme or the other, the market typically reverses course.

Volume: In trading, the number of shares that trade hands from sellers to buyers as a measure of activity.

NAMES TO KNOW

BF Skinner: An American psychologist, behaviorist, author, inventor, and social philosopher who considered free will an illusion and human action dependent on consequences of previous actions. If the consequences are bad, there is a high chance that the action will not be repeated; if the consequences are good, the actions that led to it will become more probable. Skinner called this the Principle of Reinforcement

George Soros: As an investor, Soros is a short-term speculator who makes huge bets on the direction of financial markets. He believes that financial markets can best be described as chaotic, because the prices of securities and currencies depend on human beings who are driven by emotions rather than logic.

Ivan Pavlov: A Russian physiologist known primarily for his work in classical conditioning.

Jim Cramer: The money manager and host of Mad Money on CNBC helps viewers navigate the treacherous labyrinth of Wall Street trading, recognize opportunities, and avoid pitfalls along the way. Jim is also an author. I highly recommend his series of educational books: *Confessions of a Street Addict, Real Money, Mad Money, Stay Mad for Life and Get Rich Carefully*

Larry McMillan: With more than 35 years of experience trading options, he is also well known for his educational option books and newsletters. "Options as a Strategic Investment" is one of the best-selling option books of all time and is commonly referred to as "the bible of options trading."

Leonardo Fibonacci: An Italian mathematician who recognized a sequence of numbers and ratios that constantly show up in nature. This holds true for the stock market. In a Fibonacci sequence of numbers, each number is the sum of the previous two numbers. Fibonacci began the sequence not with 0, 1, 1, 2, as modern mathematicians do, but with 1,1, 2, etc. He carried the calculation up to the thirteenth place (fourteenth in modern counting), which is 233.

Warren Buffett: Often referred to as the "Oracle of Omaha," he has led a very long, very successful career at Berkshire Hathaway as a value investor.

Acknowledgments

My family is my strength and motivation for moving ahead each and every day. Thank you to my parents for your influence and being my biggest fans, and thank you to my kids for your inspiration. I would also like to acknowledge the brilliance of Jim Cramer, who has inspired me along with millions of "Cramericans." Thank you Jim for the enormous opportunities you have given me. Stephanie Link, thank you for all of our conversations. And a big thank you to Karelyn Lambert for formatting the book. This book has been on my mind for years but truly came together after a big push from Monika Jansen and Nicole Krug, my right and left arms. Thank you ladies!

About the Authors

Bob Lang is a private trader in equity and option markets at his company, Aztec Capital LLC, and an educator through his options trading service, Explosive Options. His focus is on building strong, long-term relationships with his subscribers and making options trading for income more accessible. Using his technical expertise and a direct, hands-on approach, Bob provides time-sensitive trading information in real-time

Bob serves as one of Jim Cramer's go-to technical experts on *Mad Money* and regularly contributes to TheStreet.com. He is the proud father of two adult children and lives in Southern California

Monika Jansen is Head Kick-Ass Copywriter and Strategist at her boutique marketing agency, Jansen Communications. Her team provides copywriting and social media marketing services to small and mid-size businesses that want to grow. She started working with Bob Lang in 2013 and is continually amazed by the deep knowledge of options trading she has gained since then. Monika lives with her husband, kids, and dog in northern Virginia.

Connect with us on Social Media!

Facebook:
https://www.facebook.com/explosiveoptions/

Twitter:
https://twitter.com/aztecs99

Bob on LinkedIn:
https://www.linkedin.com/in/aztecs99/

Monika on LinkedIn:
https://www.linkedin.com/in/monikacjansen/

Can you do me a favor?

We hope you've enjoyed this book! We enjoyed writing it for you.

We would greatly appreciate your honest review on Amazon for this book. To write a review go to Amazon and select this book and write your glowing review!

Getting reviews is not so easy these days, but they help the authors immensely.

So, if you could find it in your heart to write a review, we will be eternally grateful!

Index

A

accumulation 38, 58, 61, 69
all in 25, 49, 53
analysis paralysis 43
at the money 84, 87, 89, 95, 106, 140, 141

B

back 'n fil 59
BE PATIENT 16–18
bollinger bands 35–36, 70
Buffett, Warren 9, 17, 27, 43, 49, 56–57, 64, 124

C

calendar spread 98, 101
call option 63, 72, 75, 84, 90, 91, 93, 101, 107
collar 113–14
covered call 91, 111, 114
Cramer, Jim 10, 13, 50, 165–67, 181–83
cup and handle 59

D

death cross 33–35
diagonal calendar spread 101–4
distribution 36, 69, 76
double bottom 40
double top 31
dry powder 53

E

Elliot Wave Theory 40
exchange traded fund

ETF 83, 112, 121

F

FANG 166
fat tails 36
Fibonacci, Leonardo 39–40
frequency distribution 36

G

golden cross 33
Great Recession 145, 165
Greeks 87, 90

H

historical volatility 75–77, 94–95, 104
house money 157

I

implied volatility 77, 89, 94–96, 98, 101, 104
index put options 24
intrinsic value 75, 82–84, 89, 96
IPO 158

L

leverage 1, 52, 62, 81, 83, 87, 90, 93–94, 98, 142–43, 146
liquidity 29, 56, 86, 107, 112, 138

M

macro 13
market crash 1, 124, 162
market maker 75, 138, 140
McMillan, Larry 72

N

naked call option 85, 106

O

open interest 86, 90, 107, 112
opportunity cost 17, 18
option expiration 86
options 5–10, 1–3, 5–9, 12, 21, 23, 24, 25, 26, 28, 36, 40, 52, 61–64, 71, 75–79, 81–90, 91–104, 105–14, 115, 117, 119, 137–39, 141, 145, 146
out of the money 84, 89, 96, 101, 110, 161

P

Pavlov, Ivan 27
put option 23, 26, 82, 84, 91, 94

R

risk. 5–10, 20–21, 23, 26, 31, 40, 49–53, 85, 89–90, 91–94, 97, 100–104, 105–13, 115–19, 146, 161

S

Skinner, B.F. 27
Soros, George..36, 58
stock market................1–2, 5, 9, 7–11, 23–25, 45, 55, 56, 68, 73, 82
straddle 94–98, 104
strangle 94–98, 104

T

technical analysis 9–10, 27, 35, 39–41, 125, 135, 155, 166
time value 75, 84, 88, 106
toppy 157

V

valuation 13, 65, 76, 95, 101, 119
VIX 70–71, 83, 162
volume. 13, 34, 38, 55–59, 61–63, 67, 69, 71, 86, 118, 137, 158, 170